— *Wisconsin* —
BIRD HUNTING
— TALES —

Wisconsin Bird Hunting Tales

Ken M. Blomberg

Published by The History Press
Charleston, SC
www.historypress.net

Copyright © 2018 by Kenneth M. Blomberg
All rights reserved

First published 2018

Cover art: "An Open Shot," by Ross B. Young

Manufactured in the United States

ISBN 9781467140287

Library of Congress Control Number: 2018940077

Notice: The information in this book is true and complete to the best of our knowledge. It is offered without guarantee on the part of the author or The History Press. The author and The History Press disclaim all liability in connection with the use of this book.

All rights reserved. No part of this book may be reproduced or transmitted in any form whatsoever without prior written permission from the publisher except in the case of brief quotations embodied in critical articles and reviews.

For Members of the River Bottom Bird Dog Club

*You know who you are
…and for the many dogs,
like-minded mentors, friends and
acquaintances I have met and treasured
along this long and winding trail
we call upland bird hunting.*

Contents

Preface	9
Acknowledgements	11
Introduction	13
1. Wisconsin Upland Bird Hunting	17
2. Wisconsin Upland Birds	21
3. Spirit of the Woods	30
4. In Search of Gus	36
5. An Ode to Logging Roads	41
6. Lost	45
7. A Woodcock for Maggie	52
8. Grouse Camp	59
9. The Gift	67
10. Dancing with Wolves	73
11. Secret Spots	79
12. Cycles of My Life	82
13. Puppies with No Names	86
14. Opening Days	88
15. Lenny	93
16. First Bird	98
17. Yellow Leaves and Brown Grass	102
18. Duffey	106
19. The Island	109

Contents

20. Winter Grouse Hunts	115
21. Closing Days	123
22. A Bird Dog for Baby Spraefke	130
23. Woodcock Heaven	132
24. Pheasant Hunting	135
25. Buster	139
26. On the Tail of a Storm	142
27. Dear Dr. Dean	145
28. MacQuarrie Loved Pa'tridge Hunting	148
29. Hunting the Fringes	152
About the Author	157

PREFACE

The genesis of this book can be traced back to the mid-1960s, when a friend handed me a shotgun and said, "Let's go hunting." Something I had never done before. Our quarry was birds. Non-game crows, blackbirds and pigeons. Birds on the wing. Shooting practice on private land in southeastern Wisconsin with no other objective than killing time and birds on a hot summer afternoon.

I remember late in the day laying on my back in tall grass, waiting for something to fly by. I gazed at overstuffed cumulus clouds floating by against a deep blue sky. I also recall an overwhelming wave of tranquility that day. I fell asleep, gun across my chest. Then, abruptly waking to a nearby shotgun blast. One of my buddies shot a dove. Game birds were not in season. The dove ended up on a pile of unprotected "trash" birds at the end of the day. Tranquility subsided. A sour taste in my gut materialized. Not understanding at the time, the dove's death was my first glance at hunting ethics. From the 1960s until today, my upland hunting life has evolved full circle from that humble beginning.

The purpose of this book on upland hunting is twofold. I began writing in the 1970s. My first published essay landed in a local newspaper on March 6, 1980. Hundreds, no, perhaps one thousand published articles have since appeared in newspapers and magazines, many in syndicated weekly and monthly column formats. Regular columns on the outdoors, nature, gun dogs, bird hunting and so forth. In 2017, my first book, *Up the Creek*, was published. This book is my second—with the intent to share my reflections

Preface

on hunting in Wisconsin and a fifty-year-long love affair with gun dogs and upland birds.

When you have more sunsets behind you than in front, reflecting becomes second nature. For this aging bird hunter, writing and sharing these words is therapeutic and self-serving. Hence, tranquility regained.

This book, *Wisconsin Bird Hunting Tales*, is a collection of essays that covers all corners of our state. It is not a typical where-to, how-to hunting book. But if you read between the lines, you may gather valuable information on the riches of Wisconsin's upland bird populations. A book, of course, is like a restaurant meal—and is only as good as the cook. My closest friends have reminded me more than once, "You're a better writer than a wing shooter." And several of my dogs over the years, they note, "left much to be desired."

So, join me as I reflect on hunting game birds over a lifetime in this great state of Wisconsin with my bird dogs.

Acknowledgements

This book contains original essays, and the majority are in print for the first time on these pages. A few of the pieces first appeared in one form or another in other places. They may have been revised in part and appear here with the approval of the original editors. "Spirit of the Woods," "A Woodcock for Maggie," "Grouse Camp" and "The Gift" first appeared in the *Ruffed Grouse Society* magazine. "Searching for Gus" and "Puppies with No Names" originally appeared in the *Pointing Dog Journal*. Many thanks to Matt Soberg (*RGS*) and Jake Smith (*PDJ*). A few other essays are drawn from my outdoor newspaper column "Up the Creek," which appears weekly in the *Portage County Gazette* and revised to suit these pages. Thank you Nate Enwald. And to a couple of members of the River Bottom Bird Dog Club, I give thanks: Phred and Pastor Craig for their contribution to the chapter "Lost" and Rich's poignant story "A Bird Dog for Baby Spraefke."

The painting on the cover, *An Open Shot*, is used with the kind permission of Ross B. Young. You can find more of his wonderful handiwork at rossyoung.com. The other images on the cover and throughout the book are from my private collection and include many from my son Dr. Erik J. Blomberg. A professor of wildlife at the University of Maine these days, his skills at outdoor photography bleed through on these pages. The better images jump off the page and are his.

INTRODUCTION

I remember the first ruffed grouse I missed back in 1969. I do not recall the first one I killed, but suffice it to say, it came many misses and several years later. In 1971, I shot my first woodcock. A pheasant met its match in me during the fall of 1972. A single bobwhite quail from a wild covey was my first in 1985. I've unsuccessfully hunted Hungarian partridge and sharp-tailed grouse found by my dogs by chance over the years. Today, upland bird hunters in Wisconsin primarily focus on ruffed grouse, woodcock and pheasant.

The history of upland bird hunting in Wisconsin is rich. Across the state, ghosts from the past beckon from John Muir's southcentral and western coulee country, northwest to Gordon MacQuarrie's Lake Superior south shore counties, northeast to Jean Nicolet's Chequamegon forests and closer to my home, Aldo Leopold's central forestlands. Since 1980, Park Falls has owned the undisputed title of Ruffed Grouse Capital of the World. In Hayward, MacQuarrie found grouse in abundance in and around his storied barrens covert he named the Cathedral. And let's not forget Babcock, where Leopold set up weekend grouse camps with friends, where the last wild passenger pigeon met its demise and where Wallace B. Grange wrote his classic book on grouse in 1948.

During my sixty-third year, I wrote this book's introduction. Several of the following essays and thoughts are products of my earlier writing career and reflect my bird hunting life, then and now, which spans fifty years. These days, I continue to hunt, mess around with bird dogs and write.

Introduction

Within the covers of this book is an attempt to share the musings of a bird hunter who happens to live in Wisconsin.

I was born in Chicago. My grandfather came to the city in the early 1900s by way of Escanaba in Michigan's Upper Peninsula. It was there he and his two brothers settled after crossing the ocean from Sweden. My immigrant grandparents from both sides eventually moved closer to work in Chicago and a Swedish neighborhood. My parents were born there, and my sister and I followed. Our family migrated north in 1956 when I was two years old. By twelve, we had settled in southern Wisconsin, where I was born again—surrounded by the outdoors and gun dogs.

I spent those early teenage years in the southeastern part of the state, hunting, fishing and trapping—occupations that quickly and seamlessly became a way of life. I gravitated toward like-minded outdoor friends. At eighteen, I moved "up north" with high school friends Mike and Ron. There we attended state college at Stevens Point and studied natural resource conservation. Upon graduating, Ron moved to Montana to work for the U.S. Forest Service and fight forest fires. Mike and I settled near Stevens Point. We both married, raised families and pursued careers to pay the bills—he a successful businessman and I, a water resource manager. In our spare time, we followed our passion of bird dogs and upland bird hunting. It was during those years I discovered an appetite for writing. Upland bird hunting became a way of life in the years that followed. To this day, Mike and I remain close. You will meet him and others I have collected over the years in the pages that follow—Dale, Tim, Rich and Pastor Craig, to name a few—all members of the River Bottom Bird Dog Club (RBBDC).

A few years ago, a friend called and congratulated me for being quoted in the national magazine the *Retriever Journal*. I was perplexed, as I hadn't submitted anything to that magazine. I thanked him for the heads up, went to town and picked up a copy to see for myself. There it was, alongside other quotes, pulled from a book published by Sporting Classics called *Passages: The Greatest Quotations from Sporting Literature*. I was astonished and immediately ordered a signed, deluxe copy of the book. My quote fell on page 93, between Hemingway and Burroughs. Imagine that! There it was, a 1992 quote from a monthly gun dog column I wrote for *Badger Sportsman* magazine. I tell this story not to blow my horn but to explain my affinity toward quotes from other writers—especially the greats—like Hemmingway, Hill, Leopold, Evans and Spiller. They set the bar for great

Introduction

outdoor writing. That's why I use theirs and many others from Wisconsin writers for inspiration at the beginning of all the essays in this book. Let's call it frosting on the cake, so to speak. I hope you enjoy them as much as I do—and find reading the book worth your while.

Junction City, Wisconsin
December 7, 2017

1
WISCONSIN UPLAND BIRD HUNTING

In my home state of Wisconsin, we start in mid-September. Foliage then is still so heavy that it's like hunting from inside a gunny sack. We do it though. Then come autumn's blazes of color and dazzling Indian Summer days. Muffled drummings of cock grouse again challenge and mock from the hazy hills as the leaves swirl down. Then, gray days in bleak, sometimes sodden creek bottoms. Winter's warnings in the wind. Grouse lying tight one day, spooky the next. Then snow, and grouse whirring from conifers, or swooping from popple tops, or exploding from fluffy drifts, always with that uncanny timing that can leave you agape. Good days, all of them.
—Don L. Johnson, Grouse & Woodcock: A Gunner's Guide, *1995*

The New England states historically had a reputation for outstanding upland bird hunting—due in no small part to famous outdoor writers from the past: Frank Forester, Colonel Harold P. Sheldon, Burton L. Spiller and Havilah Babcock, just to name a few. Their romantic stories of hunting New England's abandoned farms, stone fences and apple orchards captivated upland hunters at the time.

Tales of upper Great Lake states bird hunting gained momentum following the massive northern forest cutover in the 1800s. A historical marker at Rib Mountain State Park near Wausau states,

Wisconsin Bird Hunting Tales

From the 1840's to 1920's, logging overshadowed all other industries in Wisconsin. The state's northern pine forests became "pineries", providing logs to meet the nation's increasing demand for building materials. Timber cut from these pineries floated downstream as raw logs or rafts of sawn lumber. The Wisconsin River was the most treacherous of the lumber streams, and many rafts men lost their lives running logs over the rapids and whitewater.

Famous Wisconsin writers like Gordon MacQuarrie, Aldo Leopold, Mel Ellis, Dion Henderson, Jay Reed, George Vukelich, Don L. Johnson and David M. Duffey wrote of bountiful upland gunning opportunities in Wisconsin. There are others to be sure, but for my purpose, that's my list—legendary Wisconsin upland hunting writers from the past.

In the 1930s and '40s, outdoorsman Gordon MacQuarrie first wrote of bountiful upland bird, waterfowl and fishing opportunities in the Upper Great Lakes area in the *Milwaukee Journal* and several major national outdoor magazines. Aldo Leopold, in his famous *A Sand County Almanac*, shared eloquent words on ruffed grouse and woodcock hunting. They both romanced readers and lured them then and now to millions of acres of public forested lands, friendly locals and flush rates unheard of in other states.

Following suit in the 1960s and '70s, Mel Ellis, Jay Reed, Dion Henderson, George Vukelich, David M. Duffey and Don Johnson—outdoor writers for the *Milwaukee Journal Sentinel* and Madison's *State Journal*—continued in MacQuarrie's footsteps. I grew up following their stories in the newspapers and had the honor of meeting Reed, Vukelich and Johnson in person. Contemporary writers like Tom Davis, Guy De La Valdene, Steve Smith, Keith Crowley, Larry Brown and Tom Huggler continue the tradition in books and periodicals by writing about upland bird hunting in the upper Midwest.

The Great Lake states lay claim to the most expansive ruffed grouse and woodcock habitat in the world, containing the largest populations of both species. Continual timber harvest creates young growth forests, contributing to healthy upland bird populations. Wisconsin, Minnesota and Michigan have long been considered top ruffed grouse and American woodcock upland bird hunting destinations in the Midwest. Wisconsin alone has more than 1.5 million acres of public northern forests, thousands of acres of state-owned wildlife areas, southwest hardwood coulee country, wooded river bottoms and farm woodlots. Combine that with a modest native population of ring-necked pheasants in the farmland belt of southern, central and west-central Wisconsin, and our state has much to offer upland hunters.

Around the time New England was the toast of the upland crowd, loggers cut over the northern forests of Wisconsin. Farming attempts in those areas were, for the most part, failures, but resulting second growth flourished—as did young forest game birds. In 1948, Wallace Grange wrote about an abundance of ruffed grouse, common numbers of prairie chickens and sharp-tailed grouse and rare numbers of spruce grouse. Turning back the clock one hundred years, he accounted for their existence after the denuded lands healed themselves and the transition from open land to forest plant succession. Ruffed grouse, he surmised, first invades early forest succession in the thicket stage—sumac, willow, dogwood, alder, hazelnut and clumps of cherry, birch, aspen and Jack-pine. Lowland areas become densely covered with young aspen and approach small forest-like conditions. By the 1850s, ruffed grouse were considered abundant. Today, with proper forest management, including young forest growth, ruffed grouse thrive. However, prairie chickens, sharp-tail and spruce grouse remain only in scattered, limited non-hunted populations.

A scene repeated time after time as hunters go afield upland bird hunting in Wisconsin.

Pheasant hunting reached a peak back in the 1940s, '50s and '60s, when populations were at high levels in southern and central parts of the state. Today, pheasant hunting in Wisconsin centers on the southern half of the state, as well as several counties in the west-central section. Harvest rates far exceed the number of stocked birds from the state hatchery in Poynette—proving a small but resilient native population of birds in quality habitat. Many diehard local hunters enjoy great pheasant hunting, especially late in the season when birds become more concentrated in heavier cover found on federal waterfowl management areas and state-owned wildlife areas.

The current Wisconsin ruffed grouse hunting season lasts four and a half months—from mid-September to the end of January. Woodcock can be hunted from the weekend after the grouse opener until early November. Beginning in 2018, the pheasant season will run from mid-October to the first week in January. Liberal bag limits, abundant public lands and long seasons add to the allure. Wisconsin upland bird hunting is alive and well.

2
WISCONSIN UPLAND BIRDS

Wisconsin has open seasons on five upland birds: ruffed grouse, woodcock, pheasant, quail and Hungarian partridge. Here's a look at each, where they can be found and when they are in season.

RUFFED GROUSE

Of the four species of grouse found in Wisconsin, the ruffed, *Bonasa umbellus*, is the most abundant. Prairie chicken, sharp-tailed and spruce are all present in small, isolated populations with no current open hunting seasons. Years ago, all four were present in varying degrees of abundance and sought after by upland hunters. This was largely due to successional changes to Wisconsin's northern forests after being cut over in the 1800s, followed by the slash and remaining vegetation being swept over by brush fires. Young forest growth then thrived, as did the number of grouse of all stripes. Today, only the ruffed grouse remains in abundance, subject to ten-year population cycles and habitat management on private, county, state and federal forestlands.

Ruffed grouse can be found in most corners of the state, depending, of course, on suitable habitat. The Department of Natural Resources (DNR) created two zones for hunting season purposes. Zone A lies in the southeast corner of the state—east of a line drawn from Green Bay to Madison then south to the Illinois border. There the season runs from mid-October to early

December. Birds are uncommon in that zone, with only remnant populations occupying the Kettle Moraine State Forest and scattered private holdings. The rest of the state makes up Zone B, with a longer season running from mid-September to the end of January. The population gains strength north of Highway 21 on the west side of the state in the central state forests of Black River, Necedah, Meadow Valley and Sandhill. County forests north of that line have aggressive timber-harvesting programs creating young forests, edges and openings ruffed grouse depend on for survival.

It is the Northwoods of our state that holds title to the most public land open to hunting this enchanting game bird. According to the U.S. Forest Service, the combined Chequamegon-Nicolet National Forest covers more than 1.5 million acres—with the northwestern Chequamegon side of the forest covering about 858,400 acres in Ashland, Bayfield, Sawyer, Price, Taylor and Vilas Counties. The northeastern Nicolet side covers nearly 661,400 acres in Florence, Forest, Langlade, Oconto, Oneida and Vilas Counties.

State-owned land complexes include ten properties designated as state forests. These forests are generally located in the northern half of the state and total 526,948 acres. They include the Black River State Forest (68,706 acres), Brule River State Forest (46,667 acres), Coulee Experimental Forest (2,944 acres), Flambeau River State Forest (89,975 acres), Governor Knowles State Forest (20,614 acres), Northern Highland–American Legion State Forest (234,366 acres), Kettle Moraine State Forest (northern unit, 30,041 acres; southern unit, 21,315 acres), Peshtigo River State Forest (9,403 acres) and Point Beach State Forest (2,917 acres).

Wisconsin's County Forest Association (WCFA) boasts twenty-nine county forests with nearly 2.4 million acres. Together, they make up the largest public ownership in the state. According to the WCFA, their

> *ongoing sustainable timber management program on these forests provides a diversity of habitat types for a wide array of wildlife species including arguably the largest acreage of young forest habitat in the state (887,000 acres). This young forest habitat provides optimum cover and food sources for a suite of wildlife species including ruffed grouse and American woodcock. Therefore, providing Wisconsin with some of the best areas to hunt grouse or view these species in the entire country.*

The ruffed grouse has always been king of game birds in Wisconsin. Price County's Park Falls is the undisputed Ruffed Grouse Capital of the

A sign in front of city hall proclaims Park Falls, Wisconsin, the Ruffed Grouse Capital of the World.

World. Recently, a legislative bill is rumored to be circulating in Madison to name the ruffed grouse Wisconsin's state game bird alongside Wisconsin's state songbird, the robin. And out-of-staters, all the way from Georgia, Texas and both the East and West Coasts, come each fall to hunt ruffed grouse—despite where the population cycles stand. As my friend from Georgia said, "Heck, one flush an hour in a bad year up here is better than one flush a day back home!"

WOODCOCK

This migratory upland game bird inhabits all corners of our state and, I dare say, all seventy-two counties. Whether they're returning in the spring to breeding grounds or heading south in the fall, we find the American woodcock wherever suitable habitat exists. The season begins statewide in September, a week after the ruffed grouse opener, and extends until early

November. Given their widespread distribution across the state during the early season, in the words of John Alden Knight, "Woodcock are where you find them."

It is, in fact, all about habitat and access to their primary choice of food—earthworms. Woodcock know no boundaries and can be found equally distributed on private and public lands. Since earthworms prefer moist soils, hunters and their dogs would do well early in the season working saturated, moss-covered tag alder bottoms and edges of aspen clear-cuts bordered by alders. During October migrations, young successional stands of aspen, maple and birch are prime locations to explore. And if drought conditions exist, don't overlook pine plantations, where woodcock find worms under carpets of pine needles.

Woodcock hunting can be found on all public properties described above under ruffed grouse. But if it's woodcock you're after, concentrate on the county forest lands—where young succession forests are bountiful.

For the past four decades, my friend Mike and I have been mist netting male woodcock on their singing grounds in spring and capturing hens and

County forests across the state offer public hunting for woodcock and ruffed grouse on habitat management areas.

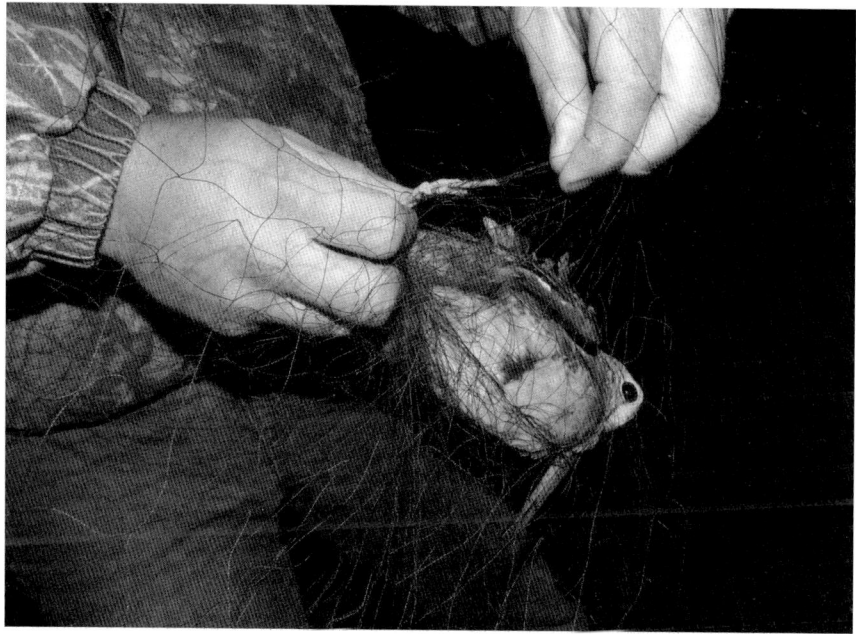

The author removes a male woodcock caught in the spring in a mist net on a singing ground.

their chicks with pointing dogs. This has transported us into a world few people enjoy. In the process, we've discovered the bird's world and ours aren't very far apart. In the field behind our house, males and females court each spring. In early May, hens walk their chicks within a stone's throw of our bird dog kennels. Mike's forty-acre property thirty miles south swarms with returning males each spring. Come fall, at dusk, birds fly above the alders bordering the edges of both our woods. The sky dancers and their mates help us live by the land.

PHEASANT

I know several upland bird hunters who seriously pursue ring-necked pheasants with their bird dogs in Wisconsin each fall. While our state is not known as a destination for this sporting game bird, it does have a sustainable, albeit modest, population of wild birds. The key, of course, is suitable habitat. According to Mark Witecha, upland wildlife ecologist with

Pheasant hunting in Wisconsin has a long tradition of wild birds and additional birds supplemented through state stocking programs.

the DNR, "Pheasants are one of the most sought-after game birds in North America, and populations do best in the agricultural landscape of southern and western Wisconsin provided there is habitat present in sufficient quantities to meet their food and cover needs throughout the year." The season for rooster pheasants begins mid-October and ends during the first week of January.

The state also maintains a game farm facility connected to the MacKenzie Center near Poynette in central Columbia County. The original hatchery built in the early 1930s is still in use today. Of the chicks hatched, some are reared on site, while others are distributed to conservation clubs participating in a day-old chick program. The state stocking program began in 1928 under the then Department of Conservation. The state continues to stock captive-raised ring-necked pheasants on public hunting grounds to boost the wild pheasant population and provide quality pheasant-hunting opportunities. In 2017, ninety-one properties were stocked with approximately seventy-six thousand pheasants from the state game farm through the end of December.

The fact that wild pheasant populations do exist in many locations of the state is substantiated by the annual statewide rooster harvest. In the 2016 pheasant hunting season alone, an estimated 43,520 hunters went out in search of pheasants and reported harvesting 307,240 birds.

A major contributing factor to those numbers is the involvement of Pheasants Forever (PF). Dedicated to "the conservation of pheasants, quail and other wildlife through habitat improvements, public awareness, education, and land management policies and programs," PF is a very active partner in the state's pheasant management programs. Headquartered in neighboring Minnesota, this national organization stresses habitat over stocking, putting most funds raised by its membership into habitat management and land purchases. PF proudly notes it has 149,000 members; a diverse staff, including more than 100 wildlife biologists; and more than 700 chapters nationwide. Wildlife habitat conservation is its mission.

Bobwhite Quail

According to the DNR's most recent surveys, "Whistling bobwhite quail routes have been conducted in Wisconsin's primary quail range since the summer of 1949. The number of routes run in 2017 was 20. The number of whistling males per stop was down in 2017 at 0.008 whistles per stop, compared to 0.016 in 2015. The number of whistling males per stop remained well below the long-term average of 0.54."

As far as the quail's future in our state, the DNR concluded:

In general, the continued declines of bobwhite quail in Wisconsin and nation-wide reflect factors beyond weather conditions. Such causative factors are thought to include habitat deterioration, predation, and possibly pesticides. Continued losses of grass lands and changes in land use threaten the future of quail populations in Wisconsin. Wild bobwhite quail exist in a few pockets of suitable habitat in Wisconsin, but are probably not going to expand their range or numbers in the current landscape composition.

The season for bobwhites begins each year in mid-October and ends during the first week of December.

Unless major changes occur that encourage the expansion of bobwhite habitat, this wonderful game bird may follow the fate of Wisconsin's Hungarian partridge and sharp-tail grouse populations.

Hungarian Partridge

The status of once abundant populations of Huns is dismal to say the least. Why there's still an open hunting season on the bird is bewildering. I suppose, like the jackrabbit a few years ago, the season will remain on the books until someone declares the species extinct in the state. I recently asked some seasoned hunters about their field observations of Huns in Wisconsin.

"I haven't seen a Hun in about eight years. There was a flock by my house that my setter used to find on our walks, but they've been gone for a while. I know southern Brown County used to have a population, but with the changes of farming practices the population is mostly gone."

"My grandparents farmed in Muskego—they had Huns, bobwhite and pheasants on their land back in the day. If I were to guess, I would say that the Huns and bobwhite were gone by the '60s."

"Up until the late '90s, early 2000s, there were huntable populations of both Huns and bobs in Lafayette County, but back then a guy could shoot ruffs there too."

"In the '60s, there used to be a covey of Huns that would show up in our yard on the south side of Waukesha when our house was the edge of town."

"Huns and pheasants were very common in western Waukesha County in the '60s—killed them all the time—then farmers started turning over their fields in the fall instead of spring, and they disappeared."

"Ken, we used to have a great Hun population in southern Brown County in my childhood, even into my early college years, the last wild Hun I shot around here was 2002. Have seen a few coveys from time to time over the last five to six years, but not huntable numbers. Wasn't there an organized hunt just for Huns around the Green Bay area in the '60s? If so, how long did it last?"

So, there you have it. There is a season for Hungarian partridge in our state, but good luck finding them. I did look up the organized Hun hunt near Green Bay and found this quote from my friend and fellow Badger outdoor writer Dan Small:

> *We were participants in the Gustav Pabst Memorial Hungarian Partridge Hunt, held in Brown County, Wis., and it was time to report back to the hunt master at the Morrison Town Hall. Later, we'd swap stories with 40 other weary hunters over a sumptuous German-style dinner at Van Abel's restaurant in nearby Holland. This event was held annually for a number of years to celebrate the sporty partridge and its introduction to Wisconsin a century ago by Gustav Pabst, the gentleman farmer of the Milwaukee brewing family.*

SHARP-TAIL GROUSE

The hunting season for sharp-tail grouse was suspended in 2017, as remnant populations in the northern barrens of the state are closely monitored by the state and the Wisconsin Sharp-tail Society.

3
SPIRIT OF THE WOODS

The season is open in the grouse woods now; the tamaracks are smoky gold and there is that same expectant hush that hangs inside an empty church. The ambience makes you want to whisper. Any sound seems an act of trespass. In the silence, the birds are hunkered down, waiting for you to make your next move, waiting for you to become so life-threatening that they will make theirs. Then they will burst from cover, scattering for their lives, almost stopping your heart in the process.
—George Vukelich, North Country Notebook, *1987*

The year was 1899. A young boy of twelve followed his father, Carl, hunting along the Mississippi River. Carl was a hunter of great local reputation during the days of year-round market hunting—with a well-developed personal code of sportsmanship. No spring waterfowl hunting for this sportsman. He never hunted after the sun went down. He set his own personal bag limits when there were none. Rand's father taught him well and started him with a single-barreled shotgun. Gun safety was paramount: "Never point a gun at anything you don't intend to kill."

In 1945, Rand, now a seasoned hunter and writer, vividly recalled shooting his first ruffed grouse. That "partridge" came after nearly two unsuccessful seasons behind his dog. The dog often treed partridge, but his father's words echoed in his head. "You may not shoot partridge from trees. You're old enough to learn wing-shooting."

> *A big partridge rose with a roar at my left…crossed behind me hell-bent for the nearest cedar swamp…a swinging shot…and the bird tumbled dead in a shower of feathers and golden leaves.*

Ethical lessons learned well indeed. Young Rand Aldo Leopold later became quite famous, and today, he is universally remembered simply as Aldo Leopold. From childhood on, Leopold was seldom without a dog at his side. His father, Carl, was a hunter of boundless integrity and, according to future Leopold graduate student Robert A. McCabe, taught his children ethics of chase and the value of wildlife. Said McCabe, "A.L. and his brothers were schooled in hunting behavior, restraint, moderation, and subtlety, a reverence for the species hunted."

Archived pictures show young Aldo, at three years of age, with a springer spaniel named Flick. A few years later, he followed the family dog into the woods—carrying a single-shot shotgun and his father's words ringing in his ears, warning him against shooting birds from trees. Leopold wrote:

> *My dog was good at treeing partridge and to forego a sure shot in the tree in favor of a hopeless one at the fleeing bird was my first exercise in ethical codes.…I could draw a map today of each clump of red bunchberry and each blue aster that adorned the mossy spot where he lay, my first partridge on the wing. I suspect my present affection for bunchberries and asters dates back to the day.*

Leopold hunted ruffed grouse and woodcock in Wisconsin. His journals well document his hunting trips across central Wisconsin and beyond. He followed German shorthairs Gus and Flick during the 1930s and '40s—right up to his untimely death at age sixty-four. He pondered and eloquently put to words why he was drawn to hunting. He defined ruffed grouse as the spirit of the north woods:

> *Everybody knows that the autumn landscape in the north woods is the land, plus a red maple, plus a ruffed grouse. In terms of conventional physics, the grouse represents only a millionth of either the mass or the energy of an acre. Yet subtract the grouse and the whole thing is dead. An enormous amount of some kind of motive power has been lost.*

That power, or "numenon" of the north woods—the ruffed grouse—represented the spirit of the region to Leopold. As a hunter and a scientist, to him, the grouse presented a form of ecological life that went above and beyond what was physical. Leopold pressed this concept to fellow scientists and encouraged them to "exercise wonder" by looking beyond contemporary science and listening to philosophers who called "this imponderable essence the numenon of material things. It stands in contradistinction to phenomenon, which is ponderable and predictable, even to the tossings and turnings of the remotest star."

Leopold wore many hats—forester, botanist, wildlife manager, writer, poet, philosopher, professor—but by all accounts, he was first and foremost a hunter. From childhood to the end of his life, he followed his family's faithful gun dogs. Late in life, many of his firsthand nature lessons were learned afield with Gus and inspired many of the essays found in his classic book, *A Sand County Almanac*, recognized worldwide as a conservation classic.

From Leopold's base camp "shack" along the Wisconsin River in Sauk County, he and Gus hunted grouse, woodcock, pheasant and quail. His extremely detailed hunting journals chronicled those hunts from the 1920s until his death in 1948. In his "Smoky Gold" essay in the *Almanac*, he wrote;

> *There are two kinds of hunting: ordinary hunting and ruffed-grouse hunting. There are two places to hunt grouse: ordinary places, and Adams County. There are two times to hunt in Adams: ordinary times and when the tamaracks are smoky gold. This is written for the luckless ones who have never stood, gun empty and mouth agape, to watch the golden needles come sifting down, while the feathery rocket that knocked them off sails unscathed into the jackpines.*

I remember missing my first grouse—standing there, mouth wide open, and watching it fly unscathed into a stand of white pines in Waushara County, one county to the east. That was more than forty-five years ago. When I first read Leopold three years later in college, I began understanding my passion for hunting—and appreciating both the hits and the misses. I paid attention to Leopold's words of wisdom in another *Almanac* essay, "Red Lanterns":

> *One way to hunt partridge is to make a plan, based on logic and probabilities, of the terrain to be hunted. This will take you to the ground where the birds ought to be. Another way is to wander, quite aimlessly, from one red lantern to another. This will likely take you where the birds actually are. The*

The Aldo Leopold "Shack" located in Sauk County served as base camp for this famous conservationist and hunter of ruffed grouse, woodcock, pheasant and quail.

> *lanterns are blackberry leaves, red in October sun....Every woodcock and every partridge has his favorite solarium under these briars. Most hunters, not knowing this, wear themselves out in the briarless scrub, and, returning home birdless, leave the rest of us in peace. By "us" I mean the birds, the stream, the dog, and myself.*

I promptly bought myself a bird dog, a pair of hunting chaps and started following stream banks—and the rest, as they say, is history. More recently, while trying to understand my own personal passion for bird hunting and that of other like-minded folks, I took the liberty of slightly modifying another of Leopold's quotes. Here, he sought to understand why wildlife helped define his role as a hunter—and how ruffed grouse connected him to the natural world:

> *To the upland hunter, the birds he seeks are the spirit of the woods and fields. Their existence does not affect the outward appearance of the uplands, but does tremendously affect our reaction toward it. Without*

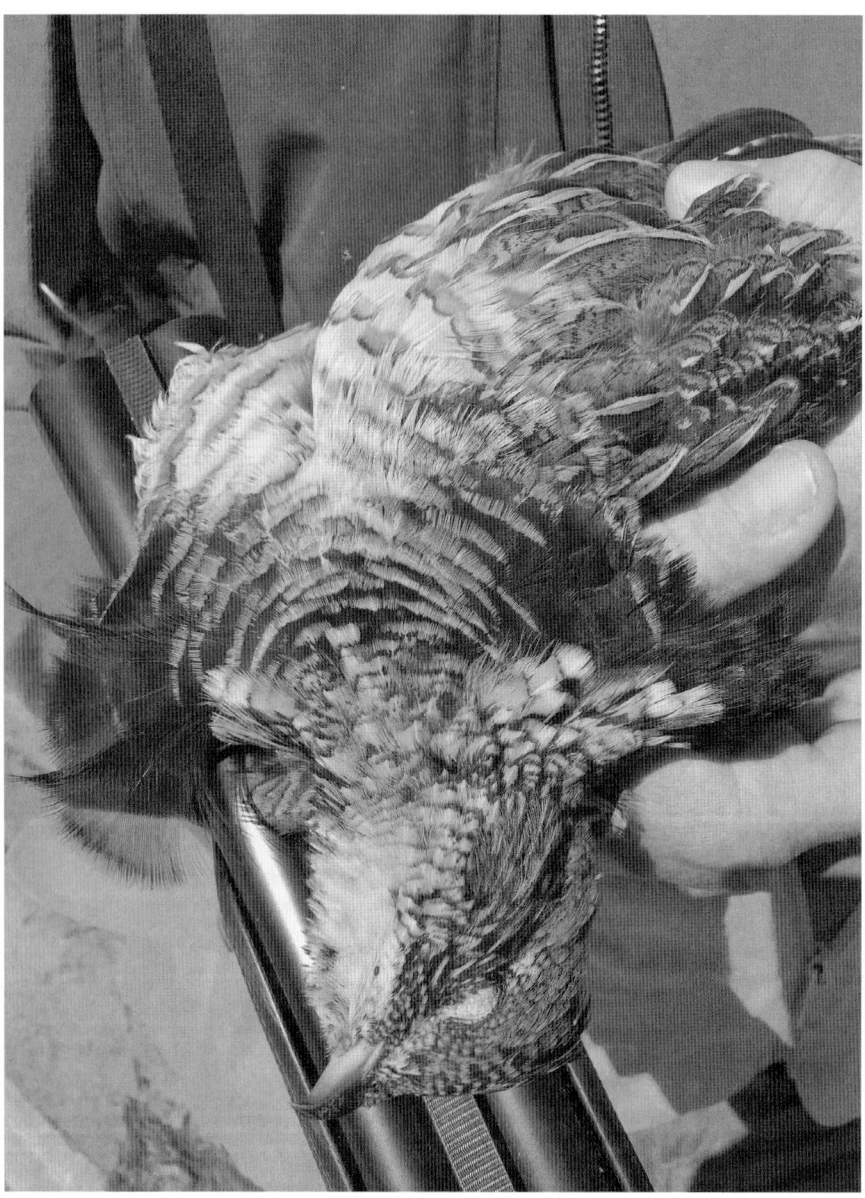

It's easy to miss ruffed grouse on the wing, but a bird in the hand is worth the effort.

whitewash in the alders, tracks in the snow, or the probability of an impending explosive flush, the uplands would be, to the bird hunter, an empty shell, a spiritual vacuum.

Ruffed grouse, per Leopold, possess the spirit of the woods, and the spirit of the woods is in the grouse. May I be so bold as to say that perhaps, when we bird hunters become part of the north woods landscape each fall, we too connect with the spirit of the woods? Who among us, when passing a good-looking covert—even at sixty-five miles per hour—intuitively know it contains the birds we chase? Why, time after time, do we instinctively know our dogs will find a bird in a likely spot along the trail? And why, oh why, when we enter the woods, do our day-to-day worries seem to mysteriously disappear?

4
IN SEARCH OF GUS

The dog knows what is grouseward better than you do. You will do well to follow him closely, reading from the cock of his ears the story the breeze is telling. When at last he stops stock-still, and says with a sideward glance, "Well, get ready," the question is, ready for what?...In this moment of uncertainty is condensed much of the virtue of grouse hunting.
—Aldo Leopold, A Sand County Almanac

This is a story about a bird dog. Not just any bird dog, but arguably one of the world's most famous bird dogs from Wisconsin. I met him more than thirty years ago in the pages of a celebrated book, *A Sand County Almanac*, written by the legendary biologist and author Aldo Leopold, who had a flair for leaving his readers with more questions than answers. I fell into his trap, yearning to know more about this legendary dog and the rest of the story.

It began on opening day of the 1936 Wisconsin pheasant hunting season, when a hunting party that consisted of Art Hawkins of the Faville Grove Wildlife Experimental Area and University of Wisconsin professors John Emlen and Aldo Leopold gathered in a farmyard in the south-central part of the state. Leading the way was a bird dog named Gus. Like countless other pheasant hunters across the landscape that day, the group anxiously looked at their watches. "I released Gus precisely at noon," recalled Art. "He quickly ranged toward a brushy fencerow and disappeared as though on the track of a pheasant."

whitewash in the alders, tracks in the snow, or the probability of an impending explosive flush, the uplands would be, to the bird hunter, an empty shell, a spiritual vacuum.

Ruffed grouse, per Leopold, possess the spirit of the woods, and the spirit of the woods is in the grouse. May I be so bold as to say that perhaps, when we bird hunters become part of the north woods landscape each fall, we too connect with the spirit of the woods? Who among us, when passing a good-looking covert—even at sixty-five miles per hour—intuitively know it contains the birds we chase? Why, time after time, do we instinctively know our dogs will find a bird in a likely spot along the trail? And why, oh why, when we enter the woods, do our day-to-day worries seem to mysteriously disappear?

4
IN SEARCH OF GUS

The dog knows what is grouseward better than you do. You will do well to follow him closely, reading from the cock of his ears the story the breeze is telling. When at last he stops stock-still, and says with a sideward glance, "Well, get ready," the question is, ready for what?...In this moment of uncertainty is condensed much of the virtue of grouse hunting.
—*Aldo Leopold,* A Sand County Almanac

This is a story about a bird dog. Not just any bird dog, but arguably one of the world's most famous bird dogs from Wisconsin. I met him more than thirty years ago in the pages of a celebrated book, *A Sand County Almanac*, written by the legendary biologist and author Aldo Leopold, who had a flair for leaving his readers with more questions than answers. I fell into his trap, yearning to know more about this legendary dog and the rest of the story.

It began on opening day of the 1936 Wisconsin pheasant hunting season, when a hunting party that consisted of Art Hawkins of the Faville Grove Wildlife Experimental Area and University of Wisconsin professors John Emlen and Aldo Leopold gathered in a farmyard in the south-central part of the state. Leading the way was a bird dog named Gus. Like countless other pheasant hunters across the landscape that day, the group anxiously looked at their watches. "I released Gus precisely at noon," recalled Art. "He quickly ranged toward a brushy fencerow and disappeared as though on the track of a pheasant."

Art had good reason to impress one of the professors, who had entrusted to him the job of managing the Faville Grove Wildlife Area near Lake Mills. The major task at hand was to census the game bird populations, which consisted of ring-necked pheasants, prairie chickens, Hungarian partridge, bobwhite quail and, during periods of migration, woodcock and snipe. "A local sportsman, Sam Kiskow, helped me get started," recollected Art. "Sam was an all-around good sportsman who raised pheasants and Canada geese in the summer and brought about the first pheasant releases in that area. He was a strong believer in winter feeding and maintained several feeding stations."

Kiskow had a bird dog, and he introduced Art to the German shorthaired pointer and Joseph Burkhart, who owned a kennel near St. Croix Falls on the Wisconsin-Minnesota border. An immigrant German gamekeeper, Burkhart, by all accounts, has been recognized as one of the all-time great GSP breeders. At the time, the breed was not very common, and breeders were extremely scarce:

> *I soon realized that a dog would be very helpful in census work, since we had four types of gamebirds in the area. Sam thought that a German pointer would be a good all-around dog for my purposes, so I contacted Burkhart. He had a dog trained on* [prairie] *chickens with a good bloodline, which he would sell for fifty dollars....* [T]*hat was a lot of money in those days. I was receiving sixty dollars per month from Aldo's lean budget.*

As it turned out, the dog with "a good bloodline" was Gotz Vom Tuebingen, son of Feldjagers Grisette and Klaus Vom Schwarenberg, universally recognized as significant imports with profound effects on the future of the breed in America. Gus, translated from his registered name, Gotz, was later bred at least twice and produced Vicki Vom Schwarenberg, who in turn produced Rusty Vom Schwarenberg. Rusty went on to become a legend as the first GSP Dual Champion in 1947. In becoming the first dual, he is now recognized as winning the first-ever American Kennel Club (AKC) Field Trial Championship. Art didn't know it at the time, but his "census dog" and hunting companion, Gus, would eventually become even more famous than his grandson Rusty. Art recalled to me, "I gave Gus to Aldo Leopold in 1938 when I moved to a job with the Illinois Natural History Survey with no way to keep a dog. Gus must have measured up to Aldo's standards because on January 20, 1944, he wrote to Burkhart as follows: 'Gus turned out to be one of the most brilliant field dogs I ever owned.'"

When Art gave his dog to Leopold, he felt it was the best gift he could think of to show his appreciation to the professor for all he had done. Years later, it occurred to him that in so doing, his present may have created problems for the professor. "Gus was not a city dog. My leaving moved him from the country into a densely-populated city—Madison. Maybe the Leopold family wasn't happy to have Gus, at least at first."

Years ago, I asked Nina Leopold Bradley, one of Aldo Leopold's daughters, about her recollections of Gus and their second GSP, Flick:

> *I'm delighted at your interest in our great dogs, Gus and Flick. They were, indeed, major parts of the Leopold family. One recollection of Gus is that between weekends at the Shack, Gus built up a great deal of energy, as he was confined to the city. Sometimes when he was let out before bedtime, he would take off, resulting in midnight telephone calls, usually from some tavern on the east side of Madison, saying, "Professor, your dog is here at my tavern, would you please come and pick him up?" You can imagine the next happening—Dad, dressing, driving, swearing, gathering up the dog.*

Aldo Leopold, now widely recognized as the father of wildlife management, was more than a hunter that opening day back in 1936. According to those who knew him well, hunting was a learning experience and his pathway into a world few others understood. Leopold shared his outdoor experiences with us all in *A Sand County Almanac*, recognized worldwide as a conservation classic. As far as I can tell, no single person, place or subject is mentioned more often in the *Almanac* than Gus. "The dog, when he approaches the briars, looks around to make sure I am within gunshot....He is the prospector of the air, perpetually searching its strata for olfactory gold. Partridge scent is the gold standard that related his world to mine."

Leopold, the professor, became the student when following Gus in the sand counties of central Wisconsin. While immersed in observing the natural world along the trail, the dog's eyes and nose instructed the hunter. I'm convinced the dogs that preceded and followed Gus brought this great conservationist and philosopher closer to the land:

> *My dog, by the way, thinks I have much to learn about partridges, and, being a professional naturalist, I agree. He persists in tutoring me, with the calm patience of a professor of logic, in the art of drawing deductions from*

Eau Pleine Rocky, a descendant of Leopold's Gus, was a favorite of the author and his family.

an educated nose. I delight in seeing him deduce a conclusion, in the form of a point, from data that are obvious to him, but speculative to my unaided eye. Perhaps he hopes his dull pupil will someday learn to smell.

From childhood on, Leopold was seldom without a dog at his side. From 1890 to 1948, Leopold had at least nine dogs, four of whom were named Flick. The nine included three spaniels, two setters, an Irish terrier and a collie; the last two, Gus and Flick, were German shorthaired pointers. And wasn't I pleased to find out my present-day shorthairs are related to Gus by way of Rusty Vom Schwarenberg. In late 1943, Art Hawkins, who at the time was serving in the military in Texas, received a copy of a manuscript, "Gus's Last Hunt from Leopold," later published in Leopold's book *Round River*. It was a sad account of losing Gus to a tragic hunting accident. But it's that opening day back in 1936 that still brought back fond memories to Art. He wanted to show off his census dog to his boss but recalled it as one of his most embarrassing moments. "He disappeared as though on the trail of a pheasant, but soon reappeared, a squealing piglet in his mouth." Ultimately, as Art recalled, "Gus redeemed himself before the day was over."

Indeed, he did. Gus went on to contribute to the foundation stock of his breed in the United States, and his extraordinary relationship with Aldo Leopold certainly contributed in bringing the world closer to the land.

5
An Ode to Logging Roads

Of all the paths you take in life, make sure a few of them are dirt.
—*John Muir*

The trail leads to nowhere. Its beginning was its end. Somewhere in between lies the answers.

My dog knows exactly where we are going. The two of us have been there many times. It's an old, overgrown logging road. At the halfway point, there is a low spot where willow and alder grow. A pocket of water, no bigger than a large bathtub, lay off to the side of the trail. Bears frequent the tub to wallow—leaving scat, tracks in the mud as reminders. And the smell. Bears stink, and we both know that smell all too well. A stump left by loggers years ago serves as a seat where I sit and ponder. The dog likes this place. Knowing we'll be there for a spell, he takes time to flounder in the tub like the bears.

The trail has no beginning and no end. A short hike from a forest service road bordering a fifty-year-old red pine plantation, it served loggers well back in the 1970s. Few people know of its existence. Rarely do many venture far from the comfort of defined graveled forest roads. I stumbled on it while grouse hunting years ago. The stump and bear wallow lure me there on occasion in the fall. Two bends in the trail containing abandoned logging landings open wide and are surrounded on the edges with thorny blackberries, alder, hawthorn and willow. Seldom do we pass without disturbing a grouse or six.

Crisscrossing the north woods of Wisconsin, logging roads are unsung heroes of our state's transportation system. Some are well defined, gated and maintained. Others are open for vehicular travel at wanderers' own risk. Many more are overgrown and disappear into maturing forests—only visible to discerning eyes of experienced hikers, woodsmen and hunters. Logging roads are, for the most part, unnamed. A few are numbered. Most lead to nowhere. Some lead to places few have ventured—some are pathways to paradise.

For north woods loggers, they represent prosperity or merely scratching out a living in a harsh, unforgiving environment. For sportsmen and women, they become pathways to favorite coverts and grouse and woodcock. For predators like bears and wolves, they are avenues through their hunting grounds.

For upland bird hunters, logging roads access habitat favored by grouse and woodcock—regenerating clear-cuts densely covered with young aspen saplings and residual plant growth—springing forth from commercial harvesting operations. Over the course of a lifetime of hunting grouse and woodcock, I have discovered the game birds I seek also prefer the company of logging roads. My dogs and I find them using the edge curbside cover as their refuge during two times of the day—late morning and late afternoon. Once the dew of the morning has burned off, the birds we seek venture into the open roadways. As chicks, young grouse find abundant insect life in the sun. Mother woodcock also lead their young there to probe the edges of puddles for worms and crustaceans.

Not long after heavy logging equipment plowed in the road to access large stands of timber, the edges, then cultivated and exposed to daylight, became nurseries for blackberry, alder, hawthorn and grasses—prime cover for upland birds and a host of other woodland songbirds. I cannot account for all the ruffed grouse I've watched burst from these edges and from under my pointers' noses or spaniels' flush. I set my clock and time my two-track walks for 10:00 a.m. and 2:00 p.m. to increase my odds. This allows for second cups of coffee in the early morning, a nap in the grass with the dog at noon and an early arrival back at camp before others hell bent on not burning daylight. I did my share of that when I wore a younger man's chaps.

Logging roads past their prime, swallowed up by time and aging forests, still serve a purpose. They stand as monuments to past forest management. They lead to areas in need of cutting. And if one becomes lost, they lead back to main roads. That was the case for me many Octobers ago while grouse and woodcock hunting with Pastor Craig an hour south of Lake

A logging road in northern Wisconsin provides access for timber harvesting and hunting.

Superior's south shore. As was his habit, he dropped me and my dog somewhere on a north–south gravel road off the beaten track at the head of a logging trail. "I'll pick you up here in an hour and a half," he said while driving off. "Or maybe two. Anyway, before dark." I waved goodbye. I checked my compass readings.

    For the next hour, my GSP dog Kane and I followed a well-defined logging road that crossed numerous other trails. Never minding my whereabouts, I knew the road back to the main road was east. So, on we hunted. A point and a miss. Another point. A woodcock and a retrieve. On to another less-defined trail at a fork in the road. As the trail slowly disappeared into tall grass and an alder swale, Kane went on point again. I left the vanishing trail to find him. A hundred yards into the woods, a grouse flushed as I passed the dog and snapped off a shot. Down went the bird, but it hit the ground running. No problem, as Kane was deft at tracking down and retrieving injured quarries. As I listened to his bell for answers, I glanced around to get my bearings. Before I could focus, back came Kane bearing our prize. I fussed over him and the bird before turning back toward our trail. One hundred

A hunter and his dog walking down a logging road gaining entrance to young forest habitat favored by grouse and woodcock.

yards of what I thought was backtracking and no trail. It had to be south, so I thought. Then I checked the compass. I had gone west. So, I traveled south by compass. Another hundred yards or so and no trail. Nothing but woods. I thought twice and turned around again to where I thought we had found the grouse. Nothing but woods is what we found. I kept going north, and as luck would have it, we crossed another major logging road I did not recognize at all. To the left was downhill. To the right and north was uphill. I chose right. Kane wanted to hunt. It was getting dark fast, so I put the dog on a leash and started walking. We emerged on an east–west gravel road and, as it turned out, a mile or more from the drop-off point. Before dark, I heard a truck coming, and bless his heart, it was Pastor.

That was many years ago. Ten to fifteen miles a day walking on trails and through the woods chasing bird dogs, woodcock and grouse is but a memory. As an aging hunter with physical limitations, logging roads have become—for the most part—the only access to the sport I love. Walking through the woods off a logging road has become an invitation to disaster. Falling and breaking something other than my pride is no longer an option. I leave that to my sons and younger hunting partners. Perhaps that's why an ode to logging roads belongs on these pages and deserves a sonnet standing for seasoned upland hunters.

6
LOST

The sun was shining when I first pushed into the tangled mass but twilight had already fallen when I finally won through to the firm ground on the other side. I have never known a more heart-breaking hour in the wilderness.
—*Burton L. Spiller,* Firelight

I first met Phred on *Upland Journal*, an online magazine and discussion forum, before face-to-face at his grouse camp up north. "You're going where?" my wife asked. "To hunt with a stranger, you found on the internet? With guns?"

"Not to worry, dear," I replied as I loaded the dogs in the truck. "He's fine, a gentleman and like-minded soul, with a passion for the uplands, bird dogs and fine guns." I was right. As a bird-hunting companion, guide and host at his cabin on a lake in the woods, I have yet to meet his equal. Our friendship grew stronger a few years later when we ventured to the prairies of Saskatchewan to hunt Hungarian partridge and sharp-tailed grouse.

"You are going where?" asked my wife again. "And with who?"

"Why, Canada, my dear. With my good friend Phred and two even finer gentlemen—Ben from the Province of New Brunswick and Don from Pennsylvania. Their names and phone numbers are hanging on the refrigerator door. And there, you will find the telephone number of the little house on the prairie where we will sleep."

"I suppose you met them on the internet, too?"

"Yes, I did. And I'll have you know their pedigrees are even superior to Phred's. These two elder statesmen of the *Upland Journal* are held in high regard across North America. Hunting with them will be a great honor for my friend Phred and me."

That, my faithful readers, is how I got to know the subject of this story. The following harrowing tale is Phred's firsthand account of becoming hopelessly lost while grouse hunting with his French Brittanys in Wisconsin's vast Chequamegon National Forest.

The following is Phred's story.

November 17, 2010

I would prefer to hand each of you a big whoopin' stick so that you can crack me in the head for being a fool, rather than to write this, but, maybe the one public service I can do is play a small part in reminding you to park your ego and use your brain before heading in to the woods. I feel fortunate to be here to write this, and it never should have come anywhere near that, but I violated the rules of common sense and nearly paid for it with more than my considerably bruised ego.

Sunday 8:15 AM

It is day two of mixed snow and rain. The woods are blanketed with wet snow and the dogs need a run. I am parked at a trail head and wearing a light shell jacket with only a couple rounds in the pocket. I am not serious about hunting, I have dressed light in the 30-degree temps and plan to walk the trail in about half an hour and then straight back out. I am attempting to fool the dogs into believing we are hunting when I am only trying to burn off their excess energy. The grouse will be holed up in the pine branches and watching us pass by underneath. Nobody knows where I decided to hunt today.

9:00 AM

The dogs are in about as far as I intend to go today and it is time to head out. Wait! I've one on point! A 100-yards or so later through a twisted maze of deadfall I hear a bird get up. I've another dog making game not far away and the first dog has chosen to dive in deeper. What follows is a half an hour of comic cluster fudge moving of birds with no shots fired.

9:45 AM

The snow and a misty sort of rain keep coming down. The clouds are right on top of the trees and there is no sun. Calm has returned to the Britts, but alarm is rising in me. My tracks twist and turn and cut back every which way. I can't find my track back to the main trail. My compass is in my vest....back at the cabin. GPS? Same place. I grabbed a light jacket for a short exercise walk with the dogs and didn't bring the vest that I wear 99.9% of the time.

9:46 AM

I call the cabin and leave a message on the answering machine that I am parked at the trail head of what we call "Labowski" and that I've gotten turned around and may need help getting out. I hope they listen to the machine when the other guys come in at lunch. I call another friend and tell him what is up. He is half an hour drive away and needs to finish what he is doing, but he will head out to follow my tracks in. No big deal.

12:00 PM

I've been wandering now, like a fool, determined to walk out. Thank God for the cell phone. I never ever bring it with me, because you can never get a signal in these woods. I now know that my friends have tried to follow and find me, but cannot make hide nor hair of where I am. And these are guys who spend a LOT of time in the woods. I've hit a creek that is in the wrong place. I shouldn't be anywhere near it, but I am. I am starting to break down physically. I am wet to the skin; my stamina has started to wane and I've got 4 hours of daylight left. Dark, which was no big deal at 10:00 AM is now something to think about. I call my friends and tell them I am going to follow the creek against the current. If it is the creek we all think it should be it cuts the road. I will be more than a mile north of where I parked, but I will be out.

1:45 PM

I've gotten caught up in a maze of feeder streams and wet lands that feed the creek. I've lost the creek and feel stuck. My friends tell me they have called the Sherriff's department rescue team. There is not enough light left for trying to figure this out on our own. I need to call 911 which will capture my GPS coordinates and they will come in and get me. I am told to stay put. Don't even think about looking for a way out once I've dialed 911 and have been locked into their GPS log.

2:00 PM

I've talked to the Sherriff's Deputy and they are coming. My cell is almost dead and I don't want it to die so I hang up. Moving was the only thing keeping me close to warm. Being in a fixed position is feeding cold and I am going hypothermic. Being still is also letting my mind go places I can't afford to let it go. The dogs sense we are in trouble and are trembling with wet, cold and perhaps fear? We need to move, but we can't leave. I decide that my odds are still pretty good for getting out, but with only two hours of light left I need to be prepared. I have no matches (vest), no food (vest) and no space blanket. The only thing I have is a Leatherman which I can use to cut pine boughs to make a shelter from the snow and rising wind. If worst comes to worst, it is the best hope the dogs and I have to share body heat through the night.

2:30 PM

The Sherriff and rescue team are there. They can't transfer GPS coordinates to their handhelds and don't want to send guys in this close to dark if they can avoid it. But they know where I am. I am way back off the nearest road according to their map. They are going to light up the siren and want me to try and walk out to the sound. Can I hear it? No. Nothing. Hang on, they will turn on more sirens. Faintly. Oh, so faintly I can hear it. It seems to be moving and bouncing off the snow-covered balsams and wind, but I've got to move.

2:31 PM

Where is Sawyer? He took off during the bough cutting. He won't come to the whistle and the locate button for his collar turns up no sound I can hear. Do I go off in the direction I last saw him? Or, do I try and walk out? I don't think I have enough time left to do both. I've got one dog still with me, but now I need to decide whether to save myself, and given how hypothermic I've become this isn't a light decision, or search for him? How do you abandon a dog?

2:45 PM

My adrenaline and sense of survival are jacked. I've hammered the whistle for 15 minutes with no response. The Sherriff has been on the phone to ask how I am coming. I haven't had the heart to tell him I haven't even left yet. Time to move. I will come back tonight and look for the dog. I've got to get out.

4:00 PM

The siren is about a 1/4 mile off now. I can hear voices from rescue guys, but there is a swamp between me and them. They direct me north to a narrowing in the swamp and wade half way out to meet me as I come across to them. They tell me my other dog came out on the road about 10 minutes ago. He is in a warm car and okay. Piper is jumping more adeptly than I from root to root and log to log. My La Crosse Burlys are full of ice water and I am wet above the knees with swamp water. Not that it matters much. The rain and snow had soaked through to skin hours ago.

4:15 PM

I am on the road. It is dark. I am out. They want to check my vitals in an ambulance. When the wave of heat from the ambulance hits me my body crashes. They keep me for the better part of an hour as my blood pressure will not come down and my pulse is racing. I am shaking so badly I can't hold an oxygen mask to my face. I want to cry, dance and break all at the same time.

3 Days Later

I am still digesting what happened. I have generally been confident while in the woods, but not cocky. I don't know how I feel today and I am still too close to it to say.

I made some mistakes that were obvious and some that were not. I left the house without the proper tools for the trip. No compass, no GPS and no survival gear. I never do that. But this time I did. This was the first day of snow and it caused me to take a coat I never wear and leave a vest I always wear. I never thought about what that meant until it was too late.

If I had stayed put, before becoming too wet and too cold, and waited for my buddies who were coming, I would have heard them yell from the main trail. Instead I let the embarrassment of being lost, and the ego to think I could get myself out, lead me very, very, very deep in exactly the wrong direction. I did watch the temps drop into the lower 20's later that night. I don't think I would have made it if I had had to spend the night in the woods. I was too wet, too cold and too ill prepared to survive. Maybe I am being over dramatic, but my gut is telling me that it would have been tight.

I went out with a plan…a short hike along a main trail…and let that plan change mid-stream without realizing the consequences. Confidence over caution? Or simply failing to think? I don't know.

I won't tell you what to do, how to hunt or what to take with you for the inevitable "what if?" But, I will ask you to think about it and to be safe.
Phred

My longtime friend and charter member of the River Bottom Bird Dog Club Pastor Craig found himself lost and alone deep in the north woods and far from home, church and friends. At least he thought so. The following is his story, as written for his northern Wisconsin congregation's newsletter.

The author's son Karl and his best friend Rocky.

Friend

You have probably heard that "A man's best friend is his dog." The bird hunting season is now open. This weekend I went on a couple very long hunts. Komet (my dog) and I went for some very long walks in search of ruffed grouse. Komet did a great job. She was hunting hard and pointed a number of birds. She was doing great, but as for me, that's another story. I couldn't hit a thing. I was out of shape. I was having a number of problems. Yet Komet didn't hold it against me!

It was on the second day of our hunt that we went on a walk that seemed would never end. In fact, it would have never ended if I didn't find a road. The only problem was I had to walk for hours to get to the truck on that road. Thirsty, hungry, and exhausted, I finally reached the truck. I opened the tailgate and let Komet into the truck. I struggled to climb into the truck to open her kennel door. As I was lying in the truck bed, Komet did something really amazing. She came out of her kennel and licked my face. It was like she was saying, "Don't worry Craig old boy, it doesn't matter that you can't hit anything. It doesn't matter that you got us lost. It doesn't matter that you are out of shape. It doesn't matter that you didn't bring us snacks. It just doesn't matter. The whole point is, it's just fun that we are together." In that one moment, Komet made my day! I realized she was truly a friend.

Think about Jesus Christ. In the upper room, He told His disciples, "No longer will I call you servants…but I have called you friends." He knew that they would desert Him. He knew that they would sin, but He also knew that He was their Savior. He loved them very much no matter what they did. He was willing to give His life for them. Like the disciples, Jesus showed His undeserved love for us.… The hymn "What a Friend We Have in Jesus" says, "Have we trials and temptations? Is there trouble anywhere? We should never be discouraged"—Take it to the Lord in prayer. Can we find a friend so faithful?

On a hunt in Sawyer County I was reminded by Komet of what it means to be a friend. Komet reminded me of Christ's underserved friendship, which also reminded me of how I should be a friend to others. Amen.

In His Name, Pastor Craig

7
A Woodcock for Maggie

Woodcock dwell on the edges of roads, clearings and streams. They are found under ferns and prefer walking on green grass. Woodcock love second-growth hardwoods, sumac, alders, old apple orchards, goldenrod and hillsides, but they are found mostly in small islands and secluded hummocks surrounded by old singing grounds. It would seem that although the birds live in seclusion, they like escape routes, or at least a nearby path of light.
—*Guy De La Valdene*, Making Game: An Essay on Woodcock, *1985*

Just like clockwork, the two met at the village café every Wednesday morning at 7:00 a.m. The cook had plates with two eggs over easy, two pieces of bacon, two slices of rye toast and coffee ready by the time they sat down. The same breakfast for both, no need to order—unless it was hunting season.

Come October, Bill added crisp hash browns to his order. "I need the extra fuel potatoes give me on a long hike," he'd say.

It was the second week of October, and a report of a cold front out of Canada had both bird hunters a bit giddy. The two old friends had been hunting together since early childhood. Tommy's father was a butcher and put in long hours—too many to allow for a leisurely pastime like hunting. Bill's father had died before he could remember. It was Tommy's Uncle Chet who took both boys under his wing early on and taught them the ropes of bird hunting and bird dogs.

By 7:30 a.m., the locals started filling the booths and front bar. Bill started to gab with one of the waitresses. Tommy squirmed in his seat. "Are you done eating? Or are we going to sit here all day chatting and drinking coffee?" he asked.

They adjourned to Bill's brand-new woody station wagon and headed north from town toward Uncle Chet's Spring Valley township farm—three miles distant. The old farmhouse sat on a ridge top. On a clear day, looking south, one could see the steeple of the Methodist church back on Main Street. The view east and west was an upland hunter's dream, a mix of farmland and woods—with several small streams draining the valleys below. An old windmill spun and creaked against a northwest wind.

Chet was sitting on his back porch when they arrived, his English setter Maggie lying at his feet. The old farmhouse had two porches, a much larger one in front. Chet preferred the back porch. "The view is much better overlooking the valley. Who in their right mind wants to look at a road when there's paradise out back to watch over?"

"I knew you two would show up today. I heard the weather forecast on the Emerson last night. Saw plenty of birds flying after sunset while sitting right here. I lost count. Should be loads out there for Maggie today. She's ready for sure!"

"The old girl didn't sleep much last night," Chet explained. "I'll bet I didn't get two good hours of sleep from her fussing and pacing all night. I swear she can sense it when a flight of woodcock are in the air."

"Considering she's been ailing of late, that might be a good thing," said Bill.

Maggie, Uncle Chet's eight-year-old English setter, had been deathly ill two months earlier. According to "Doc," she had a virus of some sort he'd never encountered before—one that medications failed to completely cure. So, for weeks, her health was up and down. She had good days and bad. Several times, the bad days appeared hopeless. More than once, Chet mentally picked her last resting spot on the farm. But that was before. This day, she greeted the arriving hunters with licks, wagging tail and a dance.

Chet explained with a smile, "She's been eating and crapping regular now for a week. Doc says she's over the hump."

Maggie was born in the spring of 1931. One of eight lively black-and-white English setter puppies, she was singled out of the litter by the breeder for potential future breeding purposes. Her blood was blue, a daughter of three-time National Bird Dog Champion Feagin's Mohawk Pal, who won the most famous of all field trials held near Grand Junction, Tennessee, in 1926, 1930 and again in 1931. But eventually, the breeder and his handler decided to place Maggie in a hunter's hands. They knew she didn't have what it took to carry on Pal's legacy.

Doc and Chet were bird hunters without a dog in 1932. Doc's male pointer died of old age the year before, and Chet's up-and-coming setter pup was tragically kicked and killed by a horse that same year. Doc knew some bird dog folks down south, and when he heard of the outstanding setter female puppy available, he arranged to have her shipped north by rail.

Chet told the boys, now grown men, the story of how he and Doc met the train at the station. "We were like two little kids waiting for Santa Claus," he recalled.

> *Doc kept looking at his pocket watch every couple of minutes until we heard the train coming into town. The conductor unloaded the wooden dog box and when we opened the door, out leaped the most beautiful black and white setter you ever laid your eyes on. She leaped into my outstretched arms and I carried her to a nearby patch of grass so she could take care of her business—after all it was a long train ride. We both stood breathlessly admiring our new pup, now five months old. I was the first to speak up. "Doc, you may have paid for her, but she's going to be living under my roof."*

Doc and Chet hunted Maggie every chance they had over the next five years. Doc survived a heart attack in November 1937 and shortly afterward closed his veterinary practice. Then, his one and only client was Maggie. He chose to no longer hunt. Chet kept hunting with Maggie, and at six years old, she was at her peak of performance. That's also when he insisted his nephew Tommy and Bill take Maggie hunting every chance they could.

"My legs ain't what they used to be," Chet lamented. "You two youngsters can do her the justice I can no longer provide, but she's going to be living under my roof."

So that's how they ended up on Uncle Chet's back porch that glorious October day. Two middle-aged men, a veteran bird dog and an eighty-five-year-old, semi-retired bird hunter. "After you two wear yourselves out following Maggie up and down the valley, maybe you'll take Maggie and me out for a short hunt around Meister's Meadow. Did I tell you there were several singing male woodcocks there last spring?"

"That sounds good, Uncle Chet. We'll hunt down to the creek, then work our way back up your south fence line. That should take a couple of hours."

"Maggie's collar and bell are hanging inside the back door on the coat rack. Take plenty of shells, and remember, don't shoot where the birds' been, shoot where they're heading! And bring me home a brace of woodcock. I have a taste for scrambled eggs and woodcock."

Tommy and Bill headed northeast from the farmhouse, following Maggie as she floated across the grassy hayfield surrounding the farm. Chet still made hay for the neighbors. He sold his last milking cow a few years after the Depression ended. He shot his only horse back in 1931.

They entered the woods by a break in the stone fence where horse-drawn wagons and tractors passed through for generations. The old wooden gate hadn't been closed for years. As younger men, they discovered the attraction partridge had for stone fences. Overgrown sections contained wild grapevines, red dogwood and cherry trees. "Dickey birds like to hunt insects on the stone fence and poop berry seeds all over the place," Uncle Chet had explained.

Sure enough, Maggie's bell went silent twenty yards beyond the opening. No words were exchanged, yet Bill stood his ground while Tommy circled wide around the frozen setter. Without warning, a hen partridge exploded from a dead oak resting on the fence. Shielded by oak branches, Tommy could not see the bird and never raised his gun. Bill, however, got a better glimpse, as the bird flew directly at his head. He instinctively ducked and, after gaining his composure, turned around just in time to pull the trigger before the bird disappeared deeper in the woods.

"Get it?" asked Tommy.

"Don't know. I did see a few feathers floating at forty yards. Let's ask Maggie."

At the shot, Maggie had broken point and immediately put her nose to the ground in the direction of the bird's flight. The men stood side by side as she worked out the mystery of a multitude of forest scents. They knew better than to disturb the shooting scene. Within minutes, Maggie had sorted things out and was very close to the spot Bill had last seen the bird fly. She disappeared for several more minutes—her bell the only thing that gave away her whereabouts. Finally, she returned, tail wagging and bird in mouth.

"Well, I'll be darned. You did hit that partridge."

"Never said I didn't—just wasn't sure how hard. Now, let's find a woodcock for Maggie," insisted Bill.

They followed the farm lane–turned–logging road downhill and toward Spring Creek. Maggie cast back and forth through the woods like she was on fire. "Pumped up by the first bird for sure," Bill noted. "She's got the energy of a two-year-old pup today."

"Uncle Chet will be glad to hear that," Tommy replied.

For a second time, Maggie's bell went silent. They found her twisted like a corkscrew under a hazelnut and dogwood copse. Again, without fanfare, the hunters took position, and one of them uttered, "Must be a woodcock, a partridge wouldn't put up with this." No sooner said and all hell broke loose. Maggie had pinned a brood of grouse—a family of seven still together in October.

With birds that close and airborne in all directions, the seasoned hunters came unglued. They emptied both barrels way too soon. Fortunately, Bill had the wherewithal to immediately reload—killing a late flusher that flew from his left to right back toward the logging road.

"We're never going to get a pair of woodcock for Maggie and Chet shooting like that," lamented Bill.

By the time they reached the creek and the scattered alders that followed its course, all three were slowing down. Maggie splashed across the creek after stopping for a drink. They followed her progress by the ringing of her bell. Suddenly, silence told the story.

Tommy was the first to speak. "She's by the spot where the small feeder creek and Spring Creek meet. You follow the fence and jump the creek upstream. I'll come in from downstream."

Just as they pictured, there she was. No national field trial champion could have looked prettier in that setting. A pointing bird dog, the colors of October, the chill in the air, the aroma and the intensity of the moment overwhelmed them both. A lone woodcock broke the spell. It rose above the alders on Bill's side of the clearing. He raised his gun slightly, but it never made his shoulder. Maggie stood fast. Tommy followed the bird's flight and squeezed off a shot before it reached the creekside cover of pine, birch and popple. Not until Tommy whispered, "OK, Maggie, fetch," did she break point.

The men admired the bird in hand as they always did. A moment of reflection was their tradition. Unspoken words were their habit. Maggie, less worried with formalities like that, was off for another bird. At least, that's what they thought.

"Can you hear her bell?"

"Yes. She's going uphill at a pretty good clip. Not sure what's got into her."

The two crossed the creek and followed her uphill. "Always trust the dog," Uncle Chet reminded them often. But Tommy thought to himself, "She's not hunting, she's heading home."

When they reached the back porch, they found Maggie lying at Uncle Chet's feet. The old man was slumped over in his favorite chair, where "no one in their right mind would look at a road when there's paradise to watch over."

A woodcock like this was all that was needed to fulfill a wish.

An hour later at the hospital in Tomah, the attending doctor told them their uncle was a lucky man. "He's had a stroke. Any longer, and it would have been much worse."

"He has a pretty little bird dog to thank for that," replied Tommy.

"And it's a good thing you finally shot straight and killed that woodcock Tommy. Otherwise we'd still be out there looking for a woodcock for Maggie," said a grinning Bill.

"Uncle Chet's in good hands now," said Tommy. "How about we take Maggie up to Meister's Meadow and shoot another woodcock. Uncle Chet will be home soon enough. And you know, it takes at least two with eggs to make his favorite breakfast."

8
GROUSE CAMP

A hunting camp is one of the few places left to us where we can dream of a near perfect tomorrow. Where the harsh realities of lost riches and faded glories can be forgotten and the dreams of what might be come down to a delightful day with not too much wind, a crisp morning silvered with frost, and finds us—at long last—with the right gun, shells, dogs and friends who will be pleased for forever to remember the day we "did it all."
—Gene Hill, *"For Better or Worse,"* Hill Country, *1978*

"Get out here!" cried Rich, the camp boss. "The wolves are howling again."

We all scrambled out of the cook's tent and stared off into the darkness. There was no wind. Stars filled the night sky. The moon was waxing crescent, and several meteors burned bright as they entered the earth's atmosphere. And sure enough, a rather large pack of timber wolves was howling in unison, straight south of camp. Wolf wailing never failed to rouse our senses—despite many years of sharing their hunting grounds.

That was on day three of a past grouse camp in northern Wisconsin. Since 1985, our group of upland bird hunters gathers for a week or two in several locations across the north woods to hunt ruffed grouse and woodcock. Together we've assembled—through three highs and four lows in the grouse cycle—through times of plenty and times of famine. That year's camp fell during a dry spell. But woodcock were plentiful. So much so that early in the week an evening feast of plucked and seasoned birds on the grill was needed to feed a hungry crew of nine hunters and avoid reaching possession limits too early in the week.

Our camp record-keeper noted harvest and flush rates of grouse were down considerably in 2013. Reports of isolated pockets of abundant birds elsewhere in the state didn't ring true for us. The ratio of woodcock to grouse flushed was ten to one. Contrast that to peaks in the cycle—like 2009 and 2010 when we encountered three times the number of grouse as woodcock.

My first invitation into this exclusive group camp came in 1996. The flyer, which I still possess, reads,

> *Each hunter is responsible for camping gear, hunting gear, food and drink. Don't forget your compass, plenty of shells and dogs. We'll hunt thousands of acres of prime grouse coverts on county forest land. To locate grouse camp, follow the map. If you cannot locate grouse camp you should probably think twice about hunting in this remote area.*

Northern Wisconsin is blessed with an abundance of public and private land open to hunting, fishing and camping—including millions of acres of federal, state, county and industrial forest land. Pitching a tent or parking a travel trailer smack dab in the middle of prime habitat is allowed on most county forest holdings. County boards struggling to balance their annual budgets aggressively harvest pulpwood for area paper mills. The result, of course, is sustainable grouse, woodcock and other forest wildlife populations well into the future.

Our camps are those of tradition. Located in remote county forest clearings at the end of unnamed roads, they are graced with canvas-walled tents. Two are placed in tandem and serve as sleeping quarters. Another single unit functions as the mess tent. Both are heated with wood stoves. A latrine consisting of a shovel and a roll of toilet paper is found out back of the tents in the woods. A new indulgence is an outdoor shower powered by a battery and positioned behind the sleeping tent.

Bird dogs can be found resting on chain gangs in the shade, sleeping in dog boxes or, in the case of a few spoiled characters like Buster—my English cocker—roaming the camp looking for handouts. However, all must behave. If a growl is heard, a favorite camp motto—coined by an elder member—is sure to follow, "I ain't paying any damn vet bills!"

Food is of upmost importance at grouse camp. Several members share the chef's hat. A couple of fellows are forbidden any attempts at cooking. All are expected to bring their share of grub. Besides grouse, woodcock,

Camp cook Tim prepares a feast of woodcock and grouse for crew at grouse camp.

Grouse camp set up along a river on county forest land in Price County.

chicken and steak on the grill, we have been treated to exotic dishes like Rich's Dutch oven delights, Colonel Dave's Georgia spaghetti surprise and Darron's Cajun shrimp and grits. Breakfast, served before the sun comes up, is a daily highlight. The aroma of coffee, bacon, sausage and eggs awakens even the soundest of sleepers—that, or cook Tim's urge to sing. Early in the week, lunch is consumed in the field. As the week wears on, most of the gang meets back at camp for a noontime meal and a nap.

Around the campfire at night, talk turns from the day's success and failures to up-and-coming dogs and puppies on the horizon. Laughter, sometimes to the point of tears, is inevitable. As embers die, several bodies around the ring disappear into the darkness of the sleeping tent. Voices lower, and discourse drifts to old dogs, the opposite sex and departed members of the camp. New this year was a short-lived religious deliberation—righteousness, churchgoing and nature's role in the matter.

Those who stay up the latest are rewarded with a sense of calm that only comes outdoors under the stars before sleep conquers the day. The feeling tugged so strong that a pair of members pulled their cots and down-filled sleeping bags outside and slept under the stars. And if we're lucky, sleep comes serenaded by lonely songs only wolves can sing.

Bird dogs resting on a chain gang on the edge of grouse camp.

The first evening of grouse camp was calm and clear, but the scattered pack started howling before dark. The wolves were half a mile away, and it sounded as if they were trying to locate one another before hunting the night away as a group. It was quite dark when they sounded off again—this time much closer. When they howled a third time, the distance from camp shortened to less than a quarter of a mile away. One lone wolf with a deeper, solemn voice seemed much closer and away from the pack. Perhaps the alpha male?

Day two was very windy, and if they howled, it was out of human earshot. I described day three at the beginning of this story.

On the morning of the fourth day, in the predawn darkness, our lone wolf—same deep, grave voice—howled a mere two hundred yards away from our tents. "Sounds like the alpha male again," commented friend Tim, a wildlife biologist and seasoned wolf researcher. That evening, he walked to the edge of the camp clearing and, with cupped hands around his mouth, raised his head toward the sky and howled. Immediately, the scattered pack sounded off.

This time, they howled continuously for five minutes. In the process, many of our bird dogs—chained out behind the tents—raised their heads and howled in response. "I think we've really got the wolves agitated this time," chuckled Tim. After dinner and drinks around the campfire, we put the dogs out of harm's way in their kennel crates before retiring for the night. Around the campfire, we all agreed, dancing with wolves at grouse camp is exhilarating.

We're no strangers to hunting in wolf country, and it seems no matter where we locate camp these days, identified wolf packs are in the area. For the past two years, our camp has been set immediately next to a wolf rendezvous site. According to the Wisconsin DNR, "Rendezvous sites are actively used from mid-May to mid-October. Rendezvous sites are generally open areas of grass or sedge adjacent to wetlands." A check of the organization's website showed we camped within a "wolf caution area" and were surrounded by "depredation sites," all within the past four years. During the days, we hunted the surrounding forest without incident. Our dogs wear bells and beepers. Between their noise, the sound of shotgun fire, whistling and talking, we are convinced wolves steer clear of our activity. Unlike bear hounds, bird dogs hunt close. The few encounters we've had over the years resulted in the wolves hightailing it deeper into the woods. Despite wolf presence, I haven't thought twice about attending past camps and those in the future. Buster, my faithful English cocker spaniel, and I eagerly await grouse camp each October.

After forty years following pointing dogs, I have taken to hunting upland birds behind flushing dogs. More specifically Buster, a field-bred English cocker who opened a whole new world to this old bird hunter. No longer physically able to penetrate deep into thick alder bottoms and young aspen clear-cuts to find my beloved German shorthairs on point, I have come to relish the close-working, enthusiastic antics of my new sidekick in the uplands.

At four years old, he had traveled with me twice to the prairies of Saskatchewan, once to the cornfields and cattails of Iowa and, of course, most corners of Wisconsin as much as possible. He will retrieve ducks and geese with all his might and leap in the air trying to grab rooster pheasant tail feathers—but his real joy is his namesake, woodcock. The scent of ruffed grouse along two-track logging roads turns him inside out. I must admit, he took to all I offered in the field without blinking an eye. Good breeding from a top-of-the-line kennel, Fallen Wings, assured the hunting instincts were there. Obedience in the home, backyard and field came without much fanfare.

He is a grouse camp fixture these days. At five months of age, he was introduced to the sounds, sights and smells of October in the Northwoods.

A typical numbered national forest road luring upland hunters into autumn splendor.

The author's son pauses and listens as his dog hunts in snow-covered grouse woods.

Left: Pastor Craig's German shorthaired pointer retrieves a grouse on a winter hunt.

Below: A plowed gravel road traversing snow-covered grouse habitat.

Opening day grouse hunters pause and praise a young German shorthaired pointer pup.

Two braces of woodcock and a pair of shotguns displayed in a layer of colorful maple leaves.

Above: The author proudly presents a grouse against elegant fall colors in all their glory.

Left: The sun peers through a brilliant array of autumn leaves.

Left: Marinated woodcock wrapped in bacon with an onion, prepared on the grill and served rare.

Below: A classic Winchester Model 21 shotgun and a winter grouse resting on a tree fungus.

Left: Son Erik with the family heirloom Winchester Model 21 shotgun over his shoulder.

Below: County forest grouse and woodcock habitat and lakes abound in northern Wisconsin.

Buster, the author's field-bred English cocker spaniel, sits atop a dog box with a brace of woodcock.

Puppies, in this case three German shorthaired pointers, anxiously await their new owners.

Left: The author's dog, Little Buck, on a trail to one of their favorite secret spots.

Below: Snowshoes come in handy to access good grouse habitat when snow depths get deep.

Right: An overgrown hunter walking trail leading to grouse and woodcock habitat far from the main road.

Below: Little Buck rests near an abandoned trailer at a secret spot cherished by the author and his sons.

Hunters tailgate lunch break in central Wisconsin on public lands managed for young forest wildlife.

Brace of pheasants on gamebag after a hunt on a public waterfowl protection area.

Pheasants on fence post bordering ideal pheasant habitat on public lands open for hunters.

One of the author's sons' dogs pointing a pheasant in late October.

A ruffed grouse drumming log—note concentrated droppings on log in front of gun.

Ideal grouse and woodcock habitat showing transition of two age classes critical for survival.

Left: Ruffed grouse tailfeathers and one of the author's favorite 28-gauge over and under shotguns.

Below: The author's son Karl and his dog Finn enter a November woods in northern Wisconsin.

Left: Son Erik's male German shorthaired pointer, a boy named Sue, sits proudly over his grouse.

Below: A December hunt produced this cinnamon-colored ruffed grouse on a state wildlife area.

Sunset over grouse camp at a county owned campground in north-central Wisconsin.

An idyllic location for grouse camp along a cascading river known for its outstanding smallmouth bass fishing.

The habitat is ideal near grouse camp along the river flowing through public county forest land.

The author holding a newborn woodcock chick he banded and released with three others and mother hen.

Buster watches camp boss Rich tend the campfire as the sun sets behind the tent.

Poking around the bird-cleaning area as a pup imprinted what Aldo Leopold described as "olfactory gold." "Partridge scent is the gold standard that relates his world to mine." Today, with eight seasons and eight grouse camps under his belt, Buster shares my passions with gusto.

Never out of shotgun range, he penetrates the thickest of cover and responds to my directions—left or right of the trail or edge of a clear-cut I might be following. That's exactly what happened one fall at a spot a few miles north of camp. Foot access to a ten-year-old clear-cut was inviting. I unloaded Buster, who in most cases rides shotgun in my truck, and proceeded down a logging road on the north end of the forty-acre cut. I slipped a pair of shells in my Ruger Red Label 28-gauge—a RGS banquet sponsor door prize by the way—and started down the trail. Before I took ten steps, I heard Buster's bell in the brush and the telltale clucking of a grouse—both ready to take flight. Sure enough, a grouse blew out of a tangle of blackberries near the gravel road and flew into the aspen stand. Before it disappeared, I managed to squeeze off a shot from the top barrel. I lost sight of the bird at the shot. We looked hard, but to no avail. Heading in the opposite direction and down the bordering trail, a second grouse took off to my left. Rising like a woodcock to the treetops, I shot and watched it tumble to the ground. Then, to my amazement, before Buster could reach the bird, it lifted off the ground and flew straight south, dangling its right leg. My gun was broke open as I fumbled to reload. By the time I gained my senses, all that was left was a Hail Mary shot and watching it fly toward the other end of the cut.

I mentioned earlier that Buster was a seasoned veteran of grouse camp. But that day in the uplands, he was still earning his stripes. I had killed many birds over flushes in his short lifespan. And like most gun dogs, he had a few more years to reach his peak—say at six or seven years old. That day and that grouse, however, moved him up the ranks a couple of notches.

We followed the path of the crippled grouse to the end of the aspen cut. It wasn't until we reached the south end that I noticed a change in the rhythm of Buster's bell. I stood my ground, and to my delight, he brought back to hand a very much alive, but crippled grouse.

That memory alone will put Grouse Camp 2013 at the top of my list of favorites.

9
THE GIFT

"Hunting ain't a competition," he said. "You ain't trying to win any prizes. Hunting is watching the dog work, and taking it easy, and shooting just enough, and walking slow, and enjoying the day."
—Robert Ruark, The Old Man and the Boy

The old man sipped his third cup of coffee and stared intently out the kitchen window. His bird dog lay at his feet. Memories drifted through his mind as he watched the sun rise over the trees bordering the training field. He daydreamed of seasons past, old hunting partners and long-departed gun dogs. He tried to forget about the phone call that morning from the doctor's office. The spell was broken when the dogs in the kennel out back began howling. The front door swung open, and his sixteen-year-old grandson stomped into the room. "Hi grandpa," he exclaimed, "Ready to go?"

The old man and the boy had hunted ruffed grouse together many times, but today's hunt would prove to be special. It was New Year's Day, and six days earlier, grandpa had promised the lad a special gift. "Put old Buck in the dog box," he instructed the youngster. "I'll go get my shotgun."

"Old Buck?" the boy thought to himself. "He died eight years ago. This is Duke, grandson of Buck. Dad must be right—the old man is getting senile."

They drove west for twenty minutes, then headed north on a gravel road for another ten until reaching a locked gate. A key in the glove compartment gave them access to an area seldom allowed to others. Beyond the gate, gravel gave way to a snow-covered logging road quickly swallowed up by a young stand of aspen trees. They pulled off the trail and parked the pickup truck between a row of pines and a small creek. "Never advertise your hotspots by parking in the open," said the old man. "Let old Buck out of his dog box, and we'll get started."

Duke stretched and relieved himself on the nearest pine before ambling off into the aspen. The old man told the boy to follow the dog while he'd walk down the trail. For the past few years, he seldom strayed off level paths. His aging legs were unsteady in the woods, and a tumble might break something, ending a hunting career in a hurry. He knew his limitations.

The dog's bell went silent off to the left side of the trail. He heard his grandson's shot, followed by a curse. With no need for further explanation, the three moved on. They followed the dog and the trail, crossing the creek twice before reaching a meadow where the path ended. It had been a forty-five-minute hike, and the elder hunter needed to rest. A rock fence bisected the field and included a large, flat boulder that made for a fine seat. From his perch, the old man could watch the dog and boy hunt the perimeter of the meadow and creek bottom. It was a spot that never failed to hold a bird or two.

The view reminded him of a Ripley print hanging on the wall back home. A framed classic, *Autumn Cover*, he purchased at a flea market—signed, framed and matted for seven bucks. "One man's junk, another's treasure," he mused.

"Why don't you take my gun for a while; it's time for this old-timer to take a break." The youngster couldn't believe his good fortune as he stared down at the old side-by-side shotgun in his hands—the family heirloom. A fine Winchester Model 21, and he was holding it for the very first time. "Hey, pay attention to Buck. He looks birdy down there by the creek."

Sure enough, the dog hit a scent cone and, with one foot in the water, stood stock-still as the boy moved in from the side. A ruffed grouse exploded from under an alder and flew left to right. The gun jumped to his shoulder, and without thinking, he swung and instinctively fired at the bird. The dog broke at the shot but, before reaching the downed bird, slammed into a second point. Meanwhile, the boy fumbled for a shell, reloaded and moved in for another flush.

This time, two birds took to the air simultaneously, one flying directly over his shoulder and back toward his grandfather, the other to the right along the stone fence. He knew better than to fire at the first bird, so he whirled around and, to his amazement, dropped the second one going straight away.

A fine double shotgun, a family heirloom, passed down and in the hands of the next generation.

"Nice shooting, boy," the old man yelled. "Two are enough, call old Buck over here and let's have a look at your birds."

The young boy's hands were still trembling when he pulled the birds from his game bag. They admired the brace of grouse for a long time, comparing the two-color phases—gray and brown—and length of the tail feathers. Both tail bands were unbroken. "Probably males," said the elder hunter. "See two spots on their rump feathers? Yep, males."

They both felt the deep satisfaction that comes with success. Grandfather and grandson had never been closer than at that moment in time. Before it ended, the old man reached into his pocket and pulled out the key to the gate.

Handing it to his grandson, he said,

> *There's your gifts for Christmas—and a New Year's wish. Promise me you won't mention this to your mother, but the doctors tell me I won't be around much longer. So, it's time for the gun and the key to be yours. Treat both with care, and if you do right by them, they'll do right by you. I wish that someday you will be able to pass them along to the next generation. And remember, when you're up here hunting with your dog, think of old Buck and me. We'll be keeping an eye on you from somewhere along this old stone fence.*

The North Dakota prairie is an easy place to ponder. It was there, while hunting pheasants and sharp-tails a few years ago, that I learned a couple of valuable lessons on giving and taking.

Gazing north, I could see the sky over Saskatchewan and a cloud of dust from an approaching vehicle. The rusty old pickup truck came to a halt just as an old man in the passenger seat rolled down his window.

"How's the hunting?" he inquired. "Finding any birds?"

I shared the story of our successful morning hunt and pointed toward the silhouettes of two others from our group on the horizon. I explained that they were working toward the next road, while I was retrieving our truck.

The old man was more interested in where we were from and how we were enjoying our hunt. After I described the hunting party, including two wildlife biologists and a preacher, he matter-of-factly responded, "I'm just a farmer."

"Just a farmer?" I thought to myself. He seemed almost apologetic.

Before going our separate ways, we talked a bit about North Dakota's generous trespass laws—un-posted lands open to hunters—and bird dogs. I made a point of thanking him for the use of his land.

"Glad to share, you out-of-state hunters are good for the local economy. Good luck to you all."

As I watched the truck disappear in its own dust, I contemplated his words. Did he realize what his generosity meant to hunters like us? Traveling to a land of plenty—turning loose the bird dogs—and that harvesting a bounty of birds on unposted private land was a dream come true. His kindness truly was a gift.

Later, when back in my home state of Wisconsin, I was reminded of something I'd taken for granted for years. A neighboring landowner had shared with my family access to his land for hunting, hiking and dog training. A small sawmill north of our place provided a livelihood for his family. Through good times and bad, Dave always carried a big smile and a cheerful greeting. He also graciously shared the gift of his land.

Access to private lands—a generous gift upland hunters should not take for granted.

Several winters ago, he clear-cut about a third of a forty-acre parcel south of our land, adjacent to one of our property's woodcock singing grounds. The resulting regenerated aspen stand will become prime nesting cover for local female woodcock and provide a backdrop for a male grouse that set up shop on a drumming log along our creek near the fence line.

Tragically, my good friend and neighbor was killed in a head-on traffic accident. But his land remains in the hands of family, and the clear-cut will stand as a memorial to his life, his land and his generosity—the greatest gift of all.

10
Dancing with Wolves

Since Day 1, I have been an outspoken advocate for, and supporter of, the DNR's wild wolf recovery program. Some cheer that. Many others do not. I don't care one way or the other about that. What I do care about is the fact Wisconsin's wolf population is now said to number about 200. So, the recovery program is working, and that, to me, is good news. The management population goal is 350. When it reaches 250, the animals will be removed from the endangered species list, which is another concern that can be taken up at the appropriate time.
—Jay Reed, "Some Problems with Wolves Are Part of the Package,"
Milwaukee Journal Sentinel, *1999*

The quote above was from a newspaper article published nearly twenty years ago. Jay Reed, an inductee to the Wisconsin Conservation Hall of Fame, was on top of the heap of outdoor writers at the time. Reed knew of which he wrote. He was reporting from Hazelhurst—where a wolf had been shot by authorities after repeatedly raiding a deer farm. I wonder what he would say today, if he had lived to see a wolf population numbering more than one thousand.

You have read and heard the reports of late. Wolves kill bear hounds. Wolves kill family dogs in their backyards. Wolf populations are growing rapidly in the Upper Midwest states of Minnesota, Wisconsin and Michigan. If you look at facts, wolves have become a real threat to domestic dogs and, in some cases, killing hunting hound dogs at an alarming rate.

Wolves, my friends, are here to stay in much of our prime grouse and woodcock coverts. That said, wolves encounter and kill some hunting dogs. Bear hounds have been hit the hardest and make up the majority of documented kills during summer training season—which coincides with wolf denning, whelping and weaning time. Bird dogs, on the other hand, enter the woods with their owners later in the summer. We've yet to see a documented instance of an upland bird dog being killed at the jaws of a wolf in the Midwest. Stalked, chased, harassed? Yes. I know of several instances firsthand—close encounters that rattled dogs and men to the core. But that is rare and, for the most part, has caused unnecessary fear among upland bird hunters.

When President Franklin D. Roosevelt coined the phrase "The only thing we have to fear is fear itself" in 1933, he wasn't talking about war or wolves—he was referring to hard economic times of the Depression. According to the experts, fear is an emotional response induced by a perceived threat and causes a change in brain and organ function—ultimately resulting in a change in behavior. The human fear response? Avoid the threat.

According to Michigan Upper Peninsula dog trainers and trialers Dennis Stachewicz and Steve Rodock, preparation, awareness and knowledge go a long way in enjoying hunting in wolf country without fear. The following are their thoughts on the matter.

"Perhaps no animal conjures up fear more than the wolf. It has been ingrained in the heads of children for years that the big bad wolf eats people in a fairy tale. The recent media and politically fueled debate over the ability to hunt wolves has led to deep-rooted debate, with seemingly no middle ground. People fear that wolves are seen as monsters that no longer fear us and are ready to devour our children, while others see them as majestic animals with more rights than people. Sadly, due to this debate, prolonged inaction until last year has led to an increase in wolf numbers in several of the Great Lakes states that has led to the death of several hounds during the recent summer training seasons and individual, mostly unconfirmed, reports of wolf scares while out with bird dogs. Regardless of your stance on the issue, the fact is that with a little bit of education and some attention to detail, you can easily continue to hunt grouse and woodcock in the Lake States without unnecessary fear or trepidation.

"Most certainly, wolves add a level of concern to deal with while hunting and especially preseason scouting and working the dogs. When hunting or, in our case, living in wolf country, we need to have a different mindset and be prepared for different concerns than you would hunting in different terrain. For example, when hunting pheasants in the open fields, we are concerned with barbed wire fences, depending on where in the country you are, poisonous snakes are a concern, and in the thick ruffed grouse and woodcock habitats logging slash and porcupines can cause you some serious and intense moments. In each of the above scenarios, we are usually prepared to deal with local condition-caused emergencies via bandages, anti-venom, etc. It is in the same manner that we should prepare to be in wolf country.

"The first things you can do are educate yourself on some basic wolf biology and habits. Things like what does a wolf track look like? The first reaction most people have when they see a wolf track is to say, 'THAT IS HUGE!!' Take your dog out to sandy and muddy areas and look closely at the size, look at the stride distance while they are trotting, running, and walking. If you can come back the next day and look at the tracks to see how they aged in the weather conditions you had, try to come back 3–5 days later; this will give you a start at guessing the age of tracks in various mediums such as sand and mud. Unless you have a 100-pound dog, many of the more common bird hunting dogs have a track that is similar in size to a coyote. Even a 120-pound lab does not have a track even close to the size of a wolf track. The track of a wolf is about 3" wide by 4" long; take a ruler and make a square that size on a piece of paper, now you have an idea of the size you are looking for. Even wolf pups of this year have large feet (plus they will be running with an adult). On your way in to the covers keep your eye open for tracks even if you are driving along at 30 mph on a 2 track a 3"x4" track can show up in soft soil.

"Wolves spend most of their day conserving as much energy as possible. They will travel down a two-track trail or opening edge, well-worn game trails and similar easier going areas while traveling, so it is always useful to check trail crossings, stop and look all directions to see if you notice any sign such as tracks or droppings. A wolf's droppings generally again are quite large and robust in diameter. At least 1" and up to 2" diameter droppings are normal, droppings full of hair and large bone pieces are common. Because of the hair and bone pieces remnants of the droppings can be seen in fall that were deposited in late spring. This is useful information because judging the frequency of travel in an area helps us decide what risk it is to hunt.

"Just like the person in the long version of the fairy tale that saves the day, the hunter can save the day with preparation. If you are coming into wolf country to hunt with your bird dog, there are some things to do that will help reduce the chances of a bad experience and will actually add to your experience by creating awareness of what is going on around you in the natural world."

More recently, Dennis had a personal encounter near his home and kennels in the woods on the outskirts of Gwinn: "I took Gabby and Georgia for a walk along CR EEA this afternoon. I was walking the road, and the girls were working both sides. Suddenly, I heard Gabby squealing terribly, and I immediately thought…snare. However, it was worse, and as I approached, I saw two wolves herding her for the kill. Imagine the horror of walking up and seeing your dog, the one that you bred, the one that you held and cut the umbilical cord on…in the scramble of her life against two savage beasts. My legs suddenly felt like they were in concrete, and a lot flashed before my eyes in those seconds. I yelled as loud as I could, and that gave Gabby an opportunity to escape when one wolf looked up at me. Gabby shot past me, and wolf number two followed, got within 10 feet of me, looked me in the eyes, and then turned and trotted into the woods. I couldn't find Gabby! Stay calm.…I gathered up Georgia and called Rebecca on the phone. She told me that Gabby was bolting up the driveway squealing and went into her kennel. I checked her over and made a visit to the vet. We couldn't find any external injuries, nor did she respond to internal checks. I will be monitoring her for internal bruising and hope she shakes this off."

I've known Dennis for years. Not much shakes him up. He served our country well in a tank division during Desert Storm. This episode gave him a new perspective on wolves and their place in the woods we share. And his military training taught him to do what is necessary to protect himself, his family and his dogs should this happen again in the future.

Steve, also from the Upper Peninsula, noted when he "was over in the Rock area doing our last training before a recent summer weekend trial, twice we had wolves howl across the road from us, probably about 200–300 yards away. Even with a couple puppies in the truck whining, they never approached us. Now we were training in a small field and could see all around so we never stopped training. The wolves were 'shock howling' to a couple of the shots. This is something that has happened to me hunting as well. Always listen after shooting."

"We talked about the wolf issue a bit at our Ruffed Grouse Society (RGS) meeting by Marquette Tuesday as well. We all had the same thought: wolves are one of the many hazards in the woods for us and our dogs. You minimize the risk you can, stay aware, then get out and enjoy the experience."

A former command officer in the Marines, Bob Priest, a West Virginia grouse hunter and frequent visitor to wolf country, is more than aware of

Encounters in the deep north woods may include wolves, more common than ever, but being prepared can avoid bad experiences.

what fear can do to the strongest of people. "Whether it is a burly Iowa farm boy, a smart aleck punk kid from Brooklyn or a kid with a bad attitude from the south side of Chicago, all will go to their knees in and cry for their mothers when fear becomes more than they can handle. Dealing with it requires being candid and honest. It means coming clean, leveling with them about risk. It also means making sure they understand how to be prepared and understanding exactly what the risk is—more importantly how to deal with it, so it gives them knowledge, then comfort that they can manage the opportunity! This last sentence is important. Many deal with the problem or the 'Opportunity' as we would say in the Marines, but not clear succinct solutions—like an ability to proceed with confidence!

"I have hunted grouse and woodcock for some sixty-three years of my life since aged nine. I have wonderful memories. However, for the first time, I see a growing threat that will impact those whom I care about: the future of grouse/woodcock hunting from the average upland hunter to those considering grouse and woodcock hunting for the first time. Just as importantly, I see the impact this is having on my friends I have made over the years—those that make a living at it—the guides, dog trainers and lodge owners. I know what those that rely on guides, stay in lodges and support dog trainers are saying and telling me privately. There is now a question among these individuals, where to go to spend their time hunting?

"In conversations with those that spend a lot of money, almost all are looking at hunting in the Lower Peninsula of Michigan, New York, New England, or out west for sharp-tails and pheasants. Some have decided not to go at all, but go to Thomasville, Georgia, or other locations like Kansas to hunt quail. Speaking to guides around the country and lodges, bookings have increased in these locations. This is my point; fear is driving people away from those that make a living at guiding, providing lodging, dog training, and the many that rely on hunters in some of the most wonderful wild bird hunting in North America, the Great Lakes region.

"I cannot speak for the bear hunter with dogs, but I know bird hunters. The bird hunter's fear they claim is more for their dogs, although if you scratch the surface, their personal safety is more than palatable in the conversations I have had."

That all said, consider that tens of thousands of upland bird hunters and their faithful gun dogs chase grouse and woodcock in wolf country daily for the better part of five months each fall and early winter and come away unscathed. Fear and trepidation are perhaps the only enemies in the north woods.

11
SECRET SPOTS

Hunts differ in flavor, but the reasons are subtle. The sweetest hunts are stolen. To steal a hunt, either go far into the wilderness where no one has been, or else find some undisturbed place under everybody's nose.
—*Aldo Leopold,* A Sand County Almanac, *1949*

Everyone needs a secret spot or two. I have a couple. No doubt, so do you.

Covert places outdoors that we can call our own fill needs within our souls. I visit one several times each fall, while following my bird dog deep into the woods northwest of our place. Suffice it to say, I cannot reveal the location—just know it is located somewhere between here and there.

The path we follow, the dog and I, leads to a place dubbed the "church of whispering pines." By any standard, the plantation is small and surrounded by younger lowland aspen and alder that for years stood tall above all else—ripe to catch the wind and speak softly to weary hunters and their dogs. The reference to the church undoubtedly came from the guilt cast from being pineward and hunting on Sunday mornings.

An hour's walk from the truck, it is a delightful place to stop and rest. A rusted trailer, long ago abandoned by loggers, sleeps besides the trail—providing a spot to lean a gun, relax tired feet and ponder. When the boys were young and toting BB guns, it doubled as a perch for aluminum can targets.

Over the span of over four decades and nine generations of dogs, I have hiked back to the Church, which is far enough in to escape all man-made sounds—except for an occasional gunshot, far off in the distance. Little Buck follows in the tracks of his ancestors, nose to the ground, searching for the scent of partridge that drifts at the mercy of the wind along the forest floor. Standing the test of time, partridge scent is what brings us to this spot each fall.

Secret spots take on names that reflect their anonymity. Tags that no one out of our close circles will understand. Like Bucky's Patch, Mallard Creek, 6-Mile Patch, Graveyard Lane, the Apple Orchard, Tower Patch and the Silo—just to name a few of mine. How about you?

For more than thirty years, a close friend and hunting buddy, Craig, has shared the Church with me. I have never met another hunter with his drive and success, and when it comes to grouse hunting, his accomplishments are that of local legend. His real secret spot is a camp up north that is about as far off the beaten path as you can go before you're on your way

A hunter heads for a secret spot he calls his own—a special place for his soul.

back out. It stands empty now—hunting at his grouse camp is on hold until further notice.

You see, Craig got his marching orders from above and is spending time in a southern seminary. In his spare moments, he still goes afield—albeit in a much different setting, but with no less passion.

In a recent message, Craig noted,

> *The other morning, while dove hunting, I was thinking of all the great opening day trips we had together....The only thing missing was the sound of the bear hounds....I told the Bible Study group that I am teaching, about that great event, but they really didn't seem to care. I guess unless you haven't had the great pleasure of enjoying a moment like that, you just don't know what you are missing....I am really starting to miss the sound, smell, taste, and friendship of grouse and woodcock hunting....Only a couple more years, God willing, and we will be able to enjoy a few more trips together...Blessings, Craig*

There are special places we have all visited in the past and secret spots that await us in the future. Here's hoping you take pleasure in yours as much as I do mine.

Craig, now known by his parishioners as Pastor Craig, has since passed the seminary with flying colors and currently resides in the north woods of Wisconsin with his wife, Janice, tending to his flock, spreading the Good Word and, in his spare time, hunting and fishing the endless out-of-doors surrounding his new home. He and I hunt and fish together whenever we can. His family stays with us during our nine-day deer rifle season around Thanksgiving. Whenever we get the chance, we spend time together at our old secret spots.

Together again, we continually seek secret spots to share and fill common needs within our souls. Everyone needs a secret spot or two. I have a couple. No doubt, so do you.

12
Cycles of My Life

> *This is superb country for deer and partridge, but I did not see many of the latter; this was a year of the few, not the many....In the low years they never disappear completely, but they require some tall walking, and singles are the common thing.*
> —Gordon MacQuarrie, "Nothing to Do for Three Weeks,"
> Stories of the Old Duck Hunters & Other Drivel

Years ago, this aging bird hunter began gauging his life span by the number of grouse cycles he'd lived through and the number he looked forward to. When you have fewer sunsets in the future than those of the past, you start thinking about such things.

I met my first ruffed grouse as a teenager in the late 1960s. It exploded from a stand of scrub oak in Waushara County and sailed off unscathed—I stood mouth open, holding an empty shotgun shell and wondering what had just happened. It was my first ruffed grouse hunt during a "high" in their ten-year population cycle, and now, forty-eight years later, I find myself looking forward to yet another high.

Ruffed grouse populations rise and fall on a ten-year cycle, and wildlife biologists agree, "In the Lake States, periods of abundance usually coincide with years ending in 0, 1 or 2, and the bottom of the depression in years ending with 5 or 6." From my personal observations, during depressed years, flush rates of one bird per hour are the norm. During a high, that will rise to five or more per hour. One memorable hunt during the high of

1980 produced twenty-five flushes during a one-hour hunt. I also noted my shooting improved during highs—was I more alert?

Reflecting on a past hunt with son Karl and Pastor Craig during a high in the cycle backs up those observations. After travel time north to camp, we were afforded enough time to get in a short, late-afternoon foray to get things started. In less than an hour, our bird dogs found two grouse, five woodcock and one very annoyed porcupine. Rocky, my son's eight-year-old German shorthair, pointed the rodent at the end of the day under a tipped-over hemlock. Luckily for all involved, Rocky backed off and chose another path back to the truck.

Day two was much more productive. We managed to see twenty-eight grouse and twenty-seven woodcock and, in the process, put enough birds in the fridge for a good meal. The day began with a late migrant loon yodeling on our lake and ended when Rocky emerged from the woods carrying a plump grouse we thought had gotten away. The value of a well-trained bird dog comes into play more than once each season, and this time was no exception.

Day three broke cold and frosty. Before we entered the woods, snow began to fall in earnest and proceeded to paint evergreens and yellow, orange and red leaves white. Snow in October is not unusual, especially near Lake Superior. And while it may have dampened our hunting clothes, it didn't our spirits. Our flush rate declined a bit, but after three days, we averaged five grouse per hour hunted.

My hunting lifespan includes five highs and five lows. My first high was in 1970. The year 2020 will be my sixth high. Statistically—based on average lifespans—I have only three highs to go: 2020, 2030, 2040. When and if I'm able to hunt at age eighty-six, you bet a high in the cycle will matter to me. But until then, I will hunt with as much gusto as I can muster, even during the lows. My dogs deserve nothing less.

Speaking of bird dogs, my wife gave me a dose of reality the other day after I shared a comment from a kennel client. This prospective buyer of an eight-week-old field-bred English cocker told me it would replace a recently deceased twenty-year-old male of the same breed. "Twenty years old!" she exclaimed. "That's it, you need to stop with new puppies for yourself. You'll die before they will, and I'll be stuck with a kennel full of orphans."

Gauging one's lifespan by the number of dogs you've owned or plan on owning is a perilous path indeed. You have your thoughts on the subject, and I have mine. Since 1974, I've owned anywhere from one to a dozen bird dogs at any given time. Owning and operating a kennel in the country helped inflate the number from time to time. Breeding, training and selling dogs

The author's son Erik manages to find a grouse or two even during a low in the cycle.

contributed to the situation. Now that I'm retired from the nine-to-five rat race, I'm trimming down my personal string of dogs. But to raise a litter or two each year to supplement my meager retirement income, I need at least a handful of dogs. Or so I tell my wife. And according to my calculations, if I have three grouse highs left in me—or twenty-one years—one more puppy shouldn't be out of the question.

Let there be no doubt, for upland bird hunters, there's nothing like a ruffed grouse high and just one more puppy.

The cyclic nature of ruffed grouse debate continues. The year this book was written ended in the number seven. According to those much more knowledgeable than me, ruffed grouse cycles in Wisconsin historically occur once in each decade, with low points of abundance in the years of each decade ending in the numeral seven, while abundance levels occur once each decade in the years ending in the numeral one. Cycle years have been precisely recorded in Wisconsin since the 1920s—with other evidence revealing numbers back to 1852.

Wallace B. Grange, in his 1948 book *Wisconsin Grouse Problems*, called upon sportsmen "who are less interested in causes than in results, the game of chance (dice) expression 'seven come eleven' is a useful memory jog, for the low of 1947 will be transformed to the abundance of 1951 almost as a matter of course." He went on to explain downswings extend for five years and highs extend up to five years—with the upcoming peak of 1951 extending from about 1949 or 1950 to about 1953. In other words—give or take a year.

Highs and lows were backed up by hunting kill indexes gathered at the time. The 1932 grouse kill in Wisconsin was 317,007, and in 1933, it was 318,410. It dropped to 131,762 in 1934 and a historic low of 72,778 birds killed in 1935. Then in 1936 and 1937, the state closed the hunting season during that decade's two low years. By the time the population rebounded in 1941–42, the kill climbed to 421,728—a historic all-time high in both populations and birds killed. Three years later, the season was closed once again for two years during the cycle's population crash in years 1945–46.

Fast forward to our current cycle. State wildlife biologists reported spring male drumming counts in 2017 across the Great Lake states were up substantially from 2016. Was the cycle on the upswing? With a good hatch, we'd be up to our eyeballs in grouse. But alas, spring and early summer weather conditions for nesting and brood rearing were disastrous. Hunters found mixed results across all three states. Only the best habitat contained good numbers for those in the right places.

Such is the nature of grouse cycles. But remember if you will Grange's saying, "seven come eleven." Our beloved ruffed grouse will be back, give or take a year.

13
PUPPIES WITH NO NAMES

But then in quick succession the days of dying were upon us....Sometimes the cardinals whistled, but very seldom. The moon still lighted up the night, but there was darkness in our hearts. We prayed and waited.
—*Mel Ellis,* Run, Rainey, Run, *1967*

Where do puppies with no names go when they die? That question crossed the old man's mind as he drove the off-road utility vehicle toward the woods.

The answer was beyond his reach, yet the question persisted. As he passed through the prairie grass field and approached the pond, he spotted a doe grazing in a food plot. He pondered the whereabouts of any fawns. After all, it was the first week of June, and one or two must be hidden nearby in the tall grass on the edge of the woods. The doe looked up, paid him no mind and returned to her morning meal.

The old man moved on, pausing for a moment near a cattail pond. A clearing at that point let the sun shine in and warmed anything in its path. He shut off the engine, leaned back and soaked in the heat. Again, he contemplated, "Where do puppies with no names go?"

Earlier that morning, after showering, he combed his hair. There, gazing back, was an old man. The aging process had really caught him off guard. Wrinkles, gray hair and worry lines replaced middle age. Where had all the years gone? Staring him in the face was a good dose of reality. An unpleasant job was at hand, and it reflected in his face.

At this stage in life, he had come to realize certain realities are self-evident. And after more than forty years of raising gun dogs, he recognized not all pregnancies and deliveries go smoothly. Sometimes there are complications. Sometimes puppies die early on. If people only knew, he pondered. Luckily, these mishaps are exceptions, not the rule. On occasion, puppies die before given a name.

Most folks are greeted by a whelping box full of lively, rambunctious pups the day they come to make their pick. Fortunately, the occasional losses occur early on. New owners are shielded—as they should be. They leave with a decade or more of joy and happiness in their arms. Breeders like the old man share in that pleasure. That makes up for the pain of occasional losses. Puppies with no names disappear like the wind. Or do they?

The trail he followed that day ended at the highest point on his property. It was a place he had buried puppies with no names in the past. Puppies with no future. Puppies that would never hear, see or smell—never put a smile on a child's face or cuddle with their littermates.

The old man put the two stillborn and one born too small and weak to survive together in a coffee can—snug and together—not unlike while in their mother's womb. He dug a hole and buried them on the hill, not far from an old ruffed grouse drumming log and next to a large white pine that served the old man well as a backstop during the recent spring turkey hunt.

He wiped the sweat from his brow and a single tear that found his cheek. Suddenly, he recalled a moment thirty years past. A visit from his parents shortly after a litter of puppies was born. A large litter—thirteen if he recalled correctly—but two died shortly after birth. He had already buried them on the hill and grumbled to his father, "What a waste."

His father was a gentle, wise man with nothing but good things to share. He wore an old man's hat that covered a balding head. "Maybe it is God's way," he said. "For every puppy that dies, there's a baby waiting in heaven. There they both grow older together waiting for the rest of us."

The old man returned to his ride and loaded the shovel. But before departing, looked to the sky, smiled and whispered, "Thanks, Dad."

14
Opening Days

September is a month of change. Headlong into the wind, the dog and I could smell the transition. Warm southerly breezes giving way to northerly drafts. We sensed the tall grasses on the trail losing the battle with time. Lush green summer vegetation was surrendering to autumn's browns, yellows and reds.

Opening day is something gun dog owners wait for all year. When the sun comes up, many will participate in a tradition that can make a grownup weak in the knees. Opening day at bird camp, to some, ranks right up there with deer or fish openers. A day dedicated bird hunters would never miss on purpose.

Often outdoor writers complain about September's early season's heavy cover, heat and mosquitoes. While it's true that the shooting can be tough and conditions can be brutal, it's a small price to pay for the chance to spend another day in the woods with our bird dogs.

Forty opening days on the same hunting grounds have come and gone, yet the anticipation still draws our gang back each autumn. Some in the group will arrive a few days early. Others will pull in just before dawn. As usual, the aroma of coffee will compete with the smell of wet dogs running around camp in the morning dew.

Someone will be showing off their new over and under shotgun, while a brand-new pup steals the show as the group starts organizing the day's hunt. With five or six in camp, planning the hunt becomes critical. Normally, woodcock hunting means two's company, three's a crowd, but on opening day, we allow for three in a party.

The woodcock will be there. A few grouse will provide additional excitement when they explode in front of our dogs' points. The dogs will find them in numbers that only opening day can provide. On that glorious morning, we will leave many more birds than we take. Opening day woodcock tend to be local, and survivors must be present to replenish the coverts next spring.

September is a month for long walks and daydreaming. A leisurely month meant for romantics like you and me. Dreaming of yesterday and yearning for tomorrow, I followed my dog along a trail to the creek.

September is a month of change. Headlong into the wind, the dog and I could smell the transition. Warm southerly breezes were giving way to northerly drafts. We sensed the tall grasses on the trail losing the battle with time. Lush green summer vegetation was surrendering to autumn's browns, yellows and reds. The neighbor's yellowing corn broadcasted the news from across the road.

Along the trail, the dog and I listened with cocked heads for the sounds of seasonal change. In this case, it was the sounds of silence. Quiet prevails in early September. We strain for but do not hear local flocks of Canada geese announcing their whereabouts. Songbirds have little to contribute. Our covey of quail, now subdued, will rejoice in chorus later this month. Robins, normally leading the musical flock each morning, are conspicuously silent. Family groups of crows fly overhead in hushed formation. Blue jays seem to be resting sore throats. The stillness is at times deafening. The occasional wailing of mourning doves or raucous call from our pileated woodpecker family are welcome diversions.

September is a month of transition. With summer shining on my backside and fall winds blowing gently in my face, it's a good month to reflect on several special occasions this year. The boss and I find ourselves at the tail end of a summer blessed with the birth of a grandson, the announcement of another grandchild to be and an upcoming family wedding. Add a new puppy to our family and another litter planned to grace our kennel this fall, and we find our good fortune cups running over.

September is a month of easygoing hunting. A dove hunt here. A duck hunt there. A goose hunt over harvested crops. Awaiting turkeys from a blind on the food plot. Woodcock and grouse hunting with best friends Mike and Dale in the popples on the Buena Vista marsh. A ruffed grouse hunt on Fort McCoy with friend Tim, his son Trent and my son Karl. And the hope for several mouthwatering game bird meals baked in the oven—served with wild rice, mushrooms and asparagus.

Come October, it'll be time to get down to business. Two duck hunting opening days: one north, one south. Grouse camp up north for a few days with Pastor Craig. A wedding in Maine, with a grouse and woodcock hunt thrown in as a present for the father of the groom. Perhaps a week-long pheasant, sharp-tailed grouse and Hungarian partridge hunt with good friends in northwest North Dakota. And finally, back to Wisconsin to hunt woodcock, grouse and ducks. That ought to wrap up a busy whirlwind month.

This will hopefully all come to pass without a hitch, but for now, it's time for a leisurely stroll in time, this first week in September. I hope yours are as fine as mine.

It's a tradition. A tradition that spans more than a decade. Opening day of Wisconsin's ruffed grouse hunting season begins for us in the forested hills west of Tomah. Another opening day with friend Tim, my son Karl and several of our upland bird dogs.

The grouse hunting season begins each year on the Saturday closest to the fifteenth of September and extends to the last day of January—138 days. That makes it one of the longest hunting seasons in our state. Only the cottontail rabbit season lasts longer—to the end of February—but grouse season ties with the squirrel hunt, which also ends at the end of January.

Like opening days of baseball, football and basketball seasons, the first golf round at area courses and the annual nine-day gun deer hunt, our grouse and woodcock openers hold special meanings to the faithful. Collectively, we are all launched into a time of the year anxiously anticipated since the curtains fell on last year's seasons. Something only those inflicted might understand. Something our non-hunting spouses know about but scratch their heads at in wonder.

Grouse hunting has a long, storied history in our state. Researchers DeStefano and Rusch tell us that in 1851, year-round hunting was ended due to intense market hunting and, from then on, restricted to four months. In 1921, due to a drastic decline in grouse populations, the season was shortened to four days. This lasted until the 1940s, when the seasons were gradually increased to today's length of four-plus months. During that time, researchers discovered ruffed grouse populations were subject to ten-year cycles that were not related to recreational hunting. The birds would recover by their own and were more dependent on proper habitat management.

In the overall scheme of things, serious grouse hunters in Wisconsin are a small group and number less than 200,000—compared to 650,000 deer hunters. The Ruffed Grouse Society (RGS), www.ruffedgrousesociety.org, is a nationally recognized federation of dedicated grouse hunters and claims 16,000 members, many calling Wisconsin home. According to RGS,

> *Our members are mainly grouse and woodcock hunters who support national scientific conservation and management efforts to ensure the future of the species. Our organization headquartered in Coraopolis, PA, employs a team of wildlife biologists to work with private landowners, and government, including local, state and federal, land managers who are interested in improving their land for ruffed grouse, American woodcock and the other songbirds and wildlife that have similar requirements.*

Our ruffed grouse opening day near Tomah resulted in nothing for dinner, but not for a lack of trying by us and a trio of German shorthaired

September upland hunting includes tall grasses on the trail, lush green woody vegetation and the tail end of summer's heat.

pointers and my trusted English cocker, Buster. Together, they found nearly thirty-five woodcock and two grouse in the moist, damp woods. One grouse ran from a point, only to run into Buster, who generously flushed it across my field of vision. You guessed it, I missed. We also entertained a horde of mosquitos and were greeted with high temperatures approaching eighty degrees by the time we left the woods and headed home at noon.

Despite the warm conditions and lack of success, we all agreed the opening day hunt was well worth the time spent. Quality time spent with family, friends, dogs and lasting memories.

15

LENNY

Right up to his death, he talked about the trip. In the end, he couldn't join us, but his spirit walked across the prairies with the dogs he so loved and the friends he cherished.

The wonderful world of upland bird hunting includes many different components, but it's the folks who share our campfires and our love of bird dogs who define us as individuals. Sadly, there's been an empty space at the River Bottom Bird Dog Club campfire for more than a decade. A charter member, Lenny, left our ranks way too soon.

Wisconsin is home for many notable professional dog trainers, several of whom gained national prominence in the past. Orin Benson, Dave Duffey and Ray Sommers are three who come to mind and may just ring a bell with you. Another, less well-known Badger gun dog trainer, Leonard Kaskavitch, touched the lives of many upland hunters and left a lasting impression to those who knew him well.

Lenny was born in Mosinee back in the 1930s and, before graduating from high school, the story goes, jumped a freight train and headed west to live the life of a cowboy. Wrangling on horseback was his dream, his passion, and he eventually became a foreman of a large cattle ranch in Montana. He remained there for many years before returning to Wisconsin, where he combined his second passion, training bird dogs, with horse training.

I met Lenny in the early '80s when he operated Sand Prairie Kennels near Mosinee. Our common love of gun dogs brought us and many other central Wisconsin bird dog enthusiasts together. This eventually led to the organization of several dog training clubs and the participation in local field trials as judges and handlers.

I remember one summer when we drove over to Shiocton to run dogs in a National Shoot to Retrieve Association (NSTRA) field trial. If I recall correctly, it was a two-day affair, with a pile of dogs entered. NSTRA trial winners are judged on a numerical basis, with the highest scores taking home the ribbons. When we arrived and checked out the running order, we found my dog paired with no other than a pointer owned and handled by nationally recognized gun dog trainer/writer Dave Duffey.

"Don't worry about the owner," Lenny assured me. "Great dogs make people famous, you better off worrying about the dog he's running."

Lenny favored English pointers; therefore, he gave me grief that my German shorthaired pointer might have trouble against Duffey's English pointer. As it turned out, Lenny was right. At the end of the day, both dogs were out of the running. His dog found more birds, but from my point of view, my dog handled much better. Years later, I read a national magazine carrying a Duffey column and learned his version of that very day. According to him, my dog was underfoot, while his handled like a dream. With all due respect to a legend, I'll leave it at that.

I spent several years training dogs under Lenny's guidance, and his way with dogs always amazed me. With horse trainer's blood running through his veins, he'd make a dog learn its lessons quickly and to the satisfaction of his long list of clients. He trained dogs for blue-collar workers as well as doctors and lawyers. He was honest with his clients and fair with the bill but never charged what he was worth.

Lenny hunted many species of game birds over his lifetime, including pheasant, ruffed grouse, woodcock and his favorite, the bobwhite quail. He spent several years living in southwestern Wisconsin near the community of Boscobel. Known today as the turkey capital of Wisconsin, Boscobel was at one time quail country, and Lenny knew every covey in the surrounding farmlands. Later in his life, he called Missouri his home, and I'd bet my best shotgun that quail had something to do with the move.

He loved woodcock for their value to a bird dog in training. As they were locally abundant and readily available, we spent many hours together working young dogs and older problem dogs on those birds in aspen and tag alders near home.

He loved killing pheasants. He traveled several times with his fellow bird dog club members to northwest North Dakota, where we stayed at friend

Doc Wilder's spacious horse ranch. On his last hunt there, he warned us we nearly killed him on a very long drive across a section of set-aside grassland. "Why didn't you boys let me post? Don't ever do that again." We all had a good laugh at his expense, but no one was laughing when we had trouble waking him up the next morning before dawn. "He looks dead. You wake him up," we all argued.

He survived the night and went out hunting with us that next day. And he lived to hunt a few more falls. Lenny died in the fall of 2003, on September 4, the day before the annual Wisconsin Woodcock Championship, a wild bird walking field trial he helped organize. That year's event was dedicated in his memory.

He left us a month before a planned October North Dakota pheasant hunting trip with his close friends—all members of the River Bottom Bird Dog Club. Right up to his death, he talked about the trip. In the end, he couldn't join us, but his spirit walked across the prairies with the dogs he so loved and the friends he cherished.

There's a group of men that I consider close upland bird hunting companions. You know, the type of companions a person can enjoy sharing campfire, lies and drinks with. While I seldom enter the woods with more than one at a time, and I occasionally hunt with others outside the core group, I'm most at ease with the members of the River Bottom Bird Dog Club (RBBDC).

Our club has only one rule and that's there are no rules. No dues, no officers, no rules. The charter members included Pastor Craig, Lenny and good friends Tim, Rich, Ray and Terry. Others joined the club over the years, whether they know it or not. I could join, they proclaimed, because I owned a gun-dog kennel, a ten-acre training field, a pond and a supply of training birds. There was room for all to camp, and on Father's Day weekend—a must date for club members to meet—all were expected to bring their children.

The bird dog club also sponsored and organized the annual Wisconsin Woodcock Championship. On the weekend before hunting seasons began in September, this wild bird field trial was held at the nearby Mead Wildlife Area along the Little Eau Pleine River in Marathon County. For

Close friends gather around campfires at night during fall hunting seasons.

eighteen years running, this popular event drew hundreds of participants and their pointing bird dogs from across the state and beyond. With blank guns and whistle, they competed to see who could locate and correctly handle, under actual hunting conditions, the most grouse and woodcock in thirty-minute braces.

For thirty years, we've carried on the RBBDC training weekend tradition. I remember when the youngest member, Little Joe, posed for a picture on top of the dog training table in diapers. That little bird dog man grew up quickly, but one recent year he missed our training weekend. He was a bit preoccupied, serving a tour of duty for the army in Iraq. I'm happy to report he's back now, safe and sound.

16
First Bird

When my father gave me the shotgun, he said I might hunt partridges with it, but that I might not shoot them from trees. I was old enough, he said, to learn wing-shooting....I could draw a map today of each clump of red bunchberry and each blue aster that adorned the mossy spot where he lay, my first partridge on the wing.
—*Aldo Leopold,* Red Legs Kicking, *1949*

In some camps, they say you never forget your first bird. In the case of ruffed grouse, I remember mine. Unfortunately, it's one I missed.

It was in the late 1960s, and I was on my first real upland bird hunt. High school friend Tim's grandfather owned an elderly German shorthaired pointer named Hans and lived in the oak and aspen forests of central Wisconsin near Westfield. Back then, most private land wasn't posted, giving us room to roam at will. And that's what we did that day, following old Hans over hill and dale.

"If you lose him, he'll find his way home." said Grandpa. "But before you do, bring me home a partridge, or two for dinner."

I don't remember much about that hunt, except for the large, brown-phased grouse that Hans flushed in front of me. The thundering roar of his takeoff nearly knocked me over, but I managed to fire a shot in his direction, just as it disappeared in the oak tree canopy.

"I think I got him!" I exclaimed.

We looked for a long time, but to no avail. Hans ran off somewhere, probably back home, and according to my hunting companions, that first grouse was no doubt alive and well.

To this day, I cannot remember when or where I killed my first grouse. But I'll never forget my first woodcock. It was a year or two later, along the banks of a small creek named Karcher in southern Wisconsin. I was hunting dogless in an area where I'd seen numerous woodcock flying at dusk. I walked right down the middle of the ankle-deep, hard-bottomed creek bed and chanced upon a woodcock probing on the bank. Up flew that little brown game bird, and when it reached the top of the aspen trees, I shot.

"I think I got him!" I exclaimed.

But I was alone, and nobody was there to hear or, for that matter, help me find the downed bird. On my hands and knees, I looked for an hour, with no luck. Sitting on the bank of the stream, head in my hands this teenage boy sat, nearly in tears.

"I know I hit that bird," I thought out loud. "It's got to be around here somewhere."

Then I heard the soft tinkle of a bird dog's bell off in the distance. As the sound got closer, I moved to the spot I knew contained my bird, protecting my kill like a predator.

"How ya doing?" asked a young boy emerging from the brush. Shortly after that, he was followed by his brother, his dad and their German wirehaired pointer.

"I lost a woodcock in here somewhere," I replied.

"Just stand back," the boy's father replied. "When you hear our dog's bell stop, he'll have located your bird.'

Sure enough, that wonderful dog accomplished in two minutes what I couldn't do in sixty. He found my first woodcock in a place I had examined minutes before. From that moment on, I was hooked on bird dogs forever. And that first woodcock became a memory lasting a lifetime.

My firsts have expanded and became more limited over the years. A new age of "firsts" began when my oldest boy, Erik, transformed into a hunter. It was his third year in the uplands, and he had shot many woodcock on the wing. Grouse, however, eluded his fledgling wing-shooting skills. We were hunting in December, a few miles from home on a large public hunting grounds in north-central Wisconsin. Buck, our eight-year-old German shorthair, had pointed a single grouse not far from our truck we both missed cleanly. About an hour later, he got birdy and pointed a bird in a fifteen-year-old aspen clear-cut.

"Walk in front of him and flush the bird," I told my son.

Before he could get near the dog, a grouse exploded from the cover, affording Erik a shot at fifteen yards, then me at twenty yards and finally

The author's son Erik, now a grown man, proudly displays a grouse taken twenty years after his first.

Erik a second try at twenty-five yards. As with my first grouse, I missed. Erik tipped the bird hard at his second shot. Despite the apparent hit, it cleared the treetops and sailed across a much larger and younger aspen clear-cut. As it flew farther, I couldn't help but notice it begin to climb upward. Higher and higher it rose as it traveled more than three hundred yards across the small valley that engulfed the clear-cut.

"That bird's hit good," I explained to my son. "Fatally hit birds sometimes fly up to abnormal heights before coming down. I once watched a woodcock fly straight up in the air one hundred feet before it died and tumbled to the ground. Mark that white birch clump across the clear-cut. That's where I saw your bird go down."

It took us more than ten minutes to cross the clear-cut and walk up to the area where I last saw his grouse. Then we put our dog to work. Like that German wirehair thirty years earlier, Buck found the gray-phased male grouse in less than two minutes, dead as a door knob.

We mounted the tail feathers of Erik's first grouse, and at the time, it hung in my office, next to the rest of our trophies from memorable hunts. A man's first bird is never forgotten, especially when he's fourteen years old.

17
Yellow Leaves and Brown Grass

Best of all he loved the fall
The leaves yellow on the cottonwoods
Leaves floating on the trout streams
And above the hills
The high blue windless skies
Now he will be a part of them forever
—Ernest Hemingway memorial inscription

I surmise we are a lot alike, you and me.

I love brown grass and yellow leaves. Green grass is for cutting. If you are like me, you have an aversion to mowing green grass during summer months. Brown grass is for lovers of the outdoors and hunters. Shorter days, longer nights and frost turn grass brown and leaves yellow. Fall colors proclaim autumn can no longer hide behind the skirt of summer.

For students of all things wild and free, the colors of fall embody October and declare a change of seasons like nothing else. So, what is it that blesses us with fall's splendor?

I know what Pastor Craig would tell me, but science suggests it's all about pigments. Green pigment production—chlorophyll—ceases as daylight wanes and temperatures drop. As chlorophyll disappears, carotenoid pigments appear, producing yellow, orange and brown colors—as do the anthocyanin pigments, which give way to red and purple colors. I prefer the good Pastor's explanation.

Tourists and nature lovers follow hunters into prime color regions and, in our state alone, spend over $1 billion per year. The best years are marked by warm, bright days and cool, crisp nights with above-freezing temperatures. Sugar production is stimulated under those conditions—making the colors and leaves hang on longer.

Buster, my English cocker spaniel, a couple of his German shorthaired pointer kennelmates and I will once again follow the trail of yellow, orange and red leaves north to grouse camp. There, we will meet up with friends embedded somewhere deep in the Douglas County forest. The colors will take my breath away. The hunting will be beyond compare. The men around the campfire—some of whom have not spoken since last year's camp—will swap stories as colorful as the woods surrounding the camp. We'll listen for howling wolves at night and follow our dogs during the day. We'll eat too much and drink just the right amount as we raise our glasses to the best time of the year.

In October, the hunter's moon will rise. According to early Native Americans—who kept track of the seasons with names for each month's full moon—"With the leaves falling and the deer fattened, it is time to hunt. Since the fields have been reaped, hunters can easily see fox and the animals which have come out to glean."

But all good things must end. The cells that attach leaves to branches dry out and block off nutrients. The winds of October will take their toll. Rain and frost will assist in the process. A colorful carpet of leaves will soon blanket the forest floors and homeowners' lawns. Grass cutting will yield to leaf raking. If left to their own accord, they will decompose under winter snow—adding nutrients to the soil and next year's lawns and gardens. I prefer to mulch them up with the final grass cuttings. The relatives call it laziness. I call it being environmentally prudent.

In the meantime, I will relish the fact that the lawnmower will soon be parked for the year and that October has arrived right on schedule—and not a moment too soon.

If the seasons of the year had flags, yellow and brown would be the colors of autumn. A bird hunter would fly the flag year-round, despite the heat, snow and grays of other seasons. A bird hunter hates mowing the green

A hunter wanders down an autumn trail covered with yellow leaves and brown grass.

grass of summer. If only the hours of summer passed by as fast as grass appears to grow, we'd find the time between Octobers to be much shorter than it seems. A bird hunter prays for a dry spell, hoping his lawn slows down and turns brown.

October finally arrives. If only the full spectrum of fall's colors lasted for months, not weeks. Imagine a calendar of dreams containing twelve months of October. Alas, time is of the essence for those of us waiting patiently this time of the year.

For hunters, that means following the course of migrant game birds. For birders, it's time to keep an eye on the sky and in the bush as early migrants are invading central Wisconsin and short-distance migrants are taking center stage statewide. American robins, rusty blackbirds and kinglets are said to be on the increase, while now is peak time for yellow-bellied sapsuckers, northern flickers and cedar waxwings. Cranes are staging. Geese and ducks are starting to move through in noisy throngs, and migrant woodcock will soon slip in—without fanfare and in the dark of night—riding waves of northerly winds. Dogwood thickets and alder bottoms become their transitory homes—their secluded whereabouts only uncovered by investigating bird dogs and hunters.

Whitetail bucks are stirring. Scrapes and rubs are magically appearing in the woods along deer trails and logging roads. While bird hunting, we find signs everywhere we go. Deer are suddenly more visible, and by the end of this month, the rut should be in full swing. Bow hunters know—their trucks and cars parked discreetly at the edge of the woods—patiently waiting in their stands for trophy bucks of a lifetime.

Tamarack and aspen will soon turn what Leopold so aptly dubbed "smoky gold," as these trees turn from yellow to gold and alder "shed their leaves" and "brambles are aglow."

October is finally here. No matter if you hunt, fish, bird watch, hike or simply enjoy a car ride in the country, now's the time to take advantage of nature's most splendid month of the year.

18

DUFFEY

Now I have more years to look back upon than there are to look forward to, but because of gun dogs and the men and women who hunt with them, I can still relish the present and have faith in the future. Training and hunting with good dogs will keep me in touch with those who share a passion for the good things in life.
—David Michael Duffey, Hunting Dog Know-How, *1983*

Thirty-some springs ago, two friends and I loaded up our bird dogs and headed east to J&H Game Farm near Shiocton. It was there we competed against sixty other handlers and their dogs in a two-day National Shoot to Retrieve Association field trial. Trucks, cars and dog trailers overflowed the gravel parking lot. Many dogs were staked out in the grass, some walked by the sides of their owners on leashes, while still others barked protest from dog crates back in scattered vehicles.

Organizers and judges stood by the clubhouse, taking in registrations and entry fees. We watched from the sidelines, taking it all in. For us, this was the big times—the Olympics of gun dog field trials. And while this was one of scores of field trials held across the state every spring and fall and only one of many we participated in and organized ourselves since, it is one that stands out prominently in my memory bank. You see, I was about to meet one of my childhood heroes in person that day.

In a cloud of dust over the gravel driveway, he suddenly appeared. His midsized pickup was pulling a large eight-hole dog trailer. A crowd of well-wishers gathered around his rig as he unloaded dogs. With a hearty belly laugh, he introduced what he called his son's attempt at a miniature German wirehaired pointer—when, in fact, it was his family's Irish terrier, Finnegan.

David Michael Duffey was his name. He was an outdoor writer, professional dog trainer, field trial judge and reporter. In reality, I had been introduced to him as a youngster on the pages of the *Milwaukee Journal* newspaper as the paper's outdoor writer and on the pages of *Outdoor Life* magazine, for which he wrote a monthly gun dog column and periodic feature articles. As it turned out, I would watch his career flourish over the years. Now described as the "Dean of Outdoor Writers," he authored nine books on hunting dogs and wrote numerous articles and columns for newspapers and sporting magazines, including the *Appleton Post-Crescent*, *Green Bay Press-Gazette*, the *American Field*, *Peterson's Hunting*, *Wing & Shot*, *Wildfowl* and, more recently, a "Question and Answers" column for *Gun Dog* magazine. He became recognized as one of the nation's leading experts on hunting dogs.

When my friends and I checked the running order that day posted on the clubhouse wall, much to my surprise, I saw my name and my dog's next to the names of Duffey and his dog. Handlers and their dogs were run in braces, and as fate would have it, I had won the lottery.

Even after all these years, I remember that thirty-minute run like it was yesterday. We shook hands, and the judges ordered us to release our dogs. His dog, an English pointer named Joe, was off like a streak—my German shorthair Kane was more reserved. Thirty minutes later, Team Duffey had racked up many more points than Team Blomberg. I didn't care. I had rubbed elbows with the best. I had met my childhood hero up close and in person. And much to my delight, six months later, he mentioned us—"the other handler and his boot-licking shorthair"—in a national magazine called *Wing & Shot*. I didn't mind his characterization. At least he remembered to mention us. And for the record, my Kane went on to win the 1990 Wisconsin Woodcock Championship.

While I only ran into Senior Duffey a few more times over the years, I did happen to strike up a friendship with his son Mike. We both were involved with an organization, the North American Versatile Hunting Dog Association (NAVHDA), and he helped me and several others organize a local chapter. The two of us journeyed to Peoria, Illinois, where we spent a weekend at a NAVHDA judge handler's clinic. Later, he helped our club train hundreds of folks and judged trials here at the local state-owned Mead Wildlife Area dog training area. He was his father's son, that's for sure—an occasional writer and a gun dog expert in his own right. On our Peoria trip, Mike shared with me a few insights about his famous father. "Yes, it is true, he's one hell of a writer. But truth be told, I'm a better dog trainer."

David Michael Duffey passed away on January 26, 2014, at age eighty-six. A celebration of his life was held at T-Dubs Irish Pub in Waupaca on February 8, 2014. Military honors were given. I was honored to attend and visit with Mike and his family. To have known Mr. Duffey—in person, in competition and through his words so skillfully applied to paper over the years—was an honor indeed.

Except for Mike, I knew no one in the packed pub. Mike took the stage and paid tribute to this exceptional man in front of the crowd. A few close family and friends followed suit. When Mike failed to get anyone else to come forward and say a few words about his father, I stood up and said this, "I'll bet nobody here recognizes me. I know Mike and have admired his father as a writer and dog man for years. I wonder if you really realize how famous he was in his world of gun dogs and outdoor writing? In that setting, this man was a rock star." I then proceeded to tell the field trial story at Shiocton and how the man was a personal inspiration to me. While my other childhood friends idolized baseball and football greats, I admired outdoor writers and dog trainers.

David Michael Duffey was, and still is, one of my favorite heroes.

19
THE ISLAND

It was not just any promise that day in October. It was not just any puppy. Rather, it was a promise, a puppy and moment in time that changed Mark's life forever.

Mark grew up on a river. Not just any river. The mighty Wisconsin River. The state's longest river. By some accounts, "the hardest working river in the world." A historic river. A river of lasting memories. A sportsmen's river. Mark's river.

Home was a mile west of the river. He hunted along the river. Fished the river at every chance. By bike, he could sit on its banks in a matter of mere minutes—any time, day or night. But it was an island on the river two miles from his home that stirred his imagination more than anything. An island that left many lasting memories. An island choked with alder and willow. An island of discovery where he met woodcock and an honest-to-goodness bird dog for the first time. Mark's island.

Locals called it Deer Island. Come deer season, families would gather together to drive the island. By boat, they'd drop two unarmed drivers on the sandy beach on the north end—then a quarter-mile south, drop off one or two more. The oldest hunters would post on the east and west high banks. On occasion, they'd jump a crafty old buck hiding from mainland hunters. The fleeing deer would instinctively swim toward either riverbank. The elder hunters knew better than to shoot a swimming deer. That they learned the hard way, years ago—when the whole hunting crew looked on in disbelief as a mighty ten-point buck sank from sight in the river's swift current—never to reappear.

Those same high banks were Mark's favorite getaway. From that perch, he spent countless hours witnessing the wonders of the natural world. There he watched nesting kingfishers come and go from nests carved in exposed soil along the high banks. Their vocal clatter—spring, summer and fall—were welcome music to his ears. From the high banks, he observed beaver, otter, ducks and geese, eagles, osprey, herons and cormorants—a never-ending wildlife parade. The passing river water was hypnotic. On calm days, it gently rolled on by. It would roar when the hydroelectric dam gates upstream were opened wide. Mark's father told him the river water was destined for the Gulf of Mexico and the oceans beyond by way of the Mississippi. "Spit in the river and imagine the journey—all the way to Louisiana."

Mark's father was a hunter of sorts. He hunted deer in November. Shot rabbits and squirrels in January with their mixed breed terrier-beagle. And if ruffed grouse got in the way, he'd add them to the bag. But his father seemed too busy farming and supporting a family the rest of the year to get serious about hunting waterfowl and upland birds. From early on, Mark read any hunting-related magazine or book he could get his hands on. He discovered on his own that some things were missing in his outdoor life.

It was a cool, overcast day late in October that Mark, then twelve years old, discovered his passion for woodcock and bird dogs. Sitting on the high banks that fateful day, he heard gunfire from the opposite side of the island. He could not see the hunters. He didn't know at what they were shooting. He heard one of the hunters call out, "Here Billy!"—followed by several blasts from a whistle. From the corner of his eye, he detected something flying low upstream along the island's edge. At a point directly across from his perch, the small brown bird ceased flying and plopped with a splash in the river. At the same time, he heard a bell. Out of nowhere, a small black-and-tan spaniel appeared and stood on the river bank like a statue. Alert and well aware of the bird flopping on the water, the dog momentarily sized up the situation—then leaped with abandon into the river's swift current.

Mark scrambled down the opposite steep bank to the river's edge. He stood and watched in amazement as the small dog swam at a precise angle to intercept the bird. Recent heavy rains had triggered a stronger than normal current, but undeterred, the dog reached his quarry. With bird in mouth, he turned back toward the island. The current sent him downstream, and Mark followed his progress by running parallel down along the riverbank. Regrettably, the dog reached shore near an overhanging tangle of brush and helplessly drifted underneath. Mark desperately watched as it struggled and became hung up in the snag. The small dog slipped underwater and out of sight.

Mark knew better. His mother had warned him to stay out of the river when he was alone. Grown men had drowned in the clutches of the river. He recalled the mighty ten-point buck sinking from sight in the river's swift current. But he knew he couldn't watch that poor hunting dog drown before his very own eyes. Mark was a good swimmer. He removed his boots and heavy clothes, stripped down to his underwear and dove into the icy October water. It took his breath away.

The island was one hundred yards away. Halfway across he felt the sting of the cold water disappear. He heard the dog thrashing and the brush shaking. Before he reached the tangle, he felt hard river bottom. The current prevented him from standing until he reached a thick branch. He spotted the dog, its belled collar hooked to an alder. Their eyes met. Mark saw desperation. The dog saw salvation. He worked his way slowly down the branch. Tugging hard twice freed the dog.

From the north end of the island, Mark heard a faint shout, "Billy, here"—followed by several blasts from a whistle. Too cold and shaking uncontrollably, he was simply not able to reply. Several minutes later, he heard a much closer, "Billy, here! Where are you, boy?" The dog, also shaking, sat at the boy's side. His head cocked as two men emerged from the woods.

"What the heck?" one of them exclaimed. The scene stopped both in their tracks. There sat a young boy, shivering and clad in wet underwear, their dog at his side and a drenched woodcock firmly held in the dog's mouth. "Where are your clothes, boy?" Mark pointed across the river. "Jim, go back and get the boat, I'll start a fire." The older man took off his hunting coat and wrapped it around Mark's shoulders. Billy stood up and shook for the first time since exiting the river.

"Good lord, Billy, you found that cripple," the man exclaimed. The dog dropped the bird in his outstretched hand. He laid it in some grass to dry, then pulled a few handfuls to fuel a fire of driftwood and grass. Soon, the fire was roaring and warming both the boy and dog. The older man lit his pipe and sat down next to them as they watched Jim rowing back from the mainland with Mark's dry clothes.

"Feel better?" he asked. "What's your name, boy?"

"Mark," he replied.

"Got a last name?"

"Johanson."
"Where do you live?"
"Three miles down River Road."

Once dry, dressed and warm, Mark retold the story to the men. "When I saw the current drag Billy underwater and the brush, I had to try and save him. He never cried out or anything. He never let go of that bird. And when we climbed out of the river, he never left my side. Not even when we heard you hollering."

"Well, young man, you apparently saved my dog's life, and for that I will always be grateful. Billy's just about the finest gun dog I've ever owned, and I've owned many over the years."

Jim dowsed the fire while the older man led the boy and dog to the boat. They crossed the river and retrieved Mark's bike from atop the high banks along River Road. Jim fired up the small outboard motor, which propelled them downstream to the public boat landing, where their truck and trailer was parked.

They were greeted at the end of the driveway by Mark's parents. The older man introduced Jim and himself—then relayed the story of their son's heroic rescue. Mark's father smiled with pride. His mother's face turned pale.

"My name is Samuel T. Perkins. I hired Jim here for the past several years to hunt woodcock on the river island north of your place. The woodcock flight is in, and they're all over the place. Billy here is wild about woodcock." The dog named Billy sat by Mr. Perkins's side, wagging his tail, looking no worse for wear.

"That's a fine-looking dog. What breed is he?"

"Billy here is a field-bred English cocker spaniel. An imported dog from the British Isles. Direct descendant of the Queen's Kennels in England, and his registered name is 'Sir William of Sandringham.' He's my once-in-a-lifetime hunting dog."

Amanda, Mark's mother, stood off to the side as the men talked, arms crossed and still distressed over her son's misadventure in the river. She did not share her husband's enthusiasm.

"I wish we could stay longer and chat, but we have several other dogs that need attention in the truck. And Jim promised me a hunt this afternoon at a covert he claims is loaded with ruffed grouse. Walk with me to the truck, would you Mr. Johanson?"

"Mark, I don't know how and when, but a reward is in your future," offered Mr. Perkins as he shook the young boy's hand and gave him a hug goodbye.

As they headed toward the truck he asked, "When's your boy's birthday?"

"The tenth of May."

"Well, this can't wait. I'd like to reward the boy for saving my dog. With your permission, I'd like to give him a puppy."

"We couldn't accept that, that's way too generous."

"You don't seem to understand. My Billy dog isn't just any dog. I am part owner of one of the largest cocker kennels in Illinois, and he is our kennel's current stud dog—seven generations out of our British and American foundation bloodlines. He fetches a handsome stud fee and is sought after by many big-name cocker breeders across the country. Had he drowned, well, I just don't care to think about it. I insist on the gift as a token reward for Mark."

Amanda, still standing off to the side, was hugging her son and scolding him at the same time when Mark's father yelled, "Amanda, could you come here for a moment?" After a short discussion, they called Mark to their sides.

"Mr. Perkins has something to show you."

The truck topper had eight ventilated compartments, four on each side. Mr. Perkins had positioned a specially designed ramp at the base of one of the dog boxes, and when he opened the door, two half-grown black-and-tan cocker puppies came rumbling down the ramp and galloped across the lawn toward Mark and his parents.

"Meet Rudy and Bo. They are brothers and sons of Billy," said Mr. Perkins.

Mark was speechless, but without prompting, he was soon running with the pups back and forth across the front yard—and ended up rolling in the grass with them in front of the adults.

After ten minutes, Mr. Perkins asked, "Mark, maybe you can help me out."

He looked up and replied, "Yes sir. What is it?"

"I need to pick one of these two fine pups for my own. If you had to pick one over the other, which would it be?"

"I guess the one that looks more like Billy, his father." Mark grabbed one and held him up. "Smaller white spot on his chest."

"That's Rudy."

"Then Rudy it is. That's the pup I'd pick if I was you Mr. Perkins."

"Well, as a matter of fact, I had my eye on Bo. Of course, I've had a lot more time to study these pups than you. Now I have a problem."

"What problem?" asked Mark.

"What to do with Rudy. I'd hate to sell him to just anyone. Do you know anyone who'd like a fine puppy like him for a hunting companion?"

Mark was speechless. He first looked at his father. Then he glanced at his mother. They were both straight-faced. Neither one of them gave him a clue. He knew they could not afford such an expensive puppy. He looked back to Mr. Perkins, bowed his head and said, "No sir, I do not."

"How about if I leave him here with you?"

Mark was stunned. He looked at his parents, who were both smiling. His eyes welled up with tears, and he squeezed Rudy tightly to his chest.

"Really? You're not kidding me are you? Mom? Dad? Are you sure?"

They both nodded their approval as Mr. Perkins went on to say, "Here's the deal young man. You earned this pup the moment you pulled his daddy from the river this morning. He's your reward. But it comes to you with a sincere promise to your folks and me. You must promise to take on total responsibility for Rudy's well-being. And should the time come that I'd like to use him in our kennel's breeding program, I reserve that right. That is, if you do your job in making him a top-notch hunting dog. Think you're up to that?"

"Yes sir, I am. I promise."

It was not just any promise that day in October. It was not just any puppy. Rather, it was a promise, a puppy and moment in time that changed Mark's life forever.

20
Winter Grouse Hunts

Gone are the golden days of autumn, as lush foliage has been replaced by snow, naked trees and chill arctic winds. Walking takes on new meaning when snow reaches the top of one's boots—no longer are hunts a casual stroll through the woods. Grouse have taken to sleeping in snow banks and feeding on the sly, early and late in the day. To do otherwise would likely prove fatal.

Hunting ruffed grouse during winter months is not for the faint of heart. Some years are forgiving, with minimal snow cover affording hunters and their bird dogs smooth going—but other years deliver abundant snowfall and reasons enough to put a damper on grouse hunting. Either way, winter grouse hunting is a favorite pastime for many northern upland bird hunters.

Strolling along colorful game trails in October seems a distant memory when snow depths range from eight to sixteen inches, north and south. Good old-fashioned Wisconsin winters happen. The white stuff—drifting knee-deep in places—will turn away even the heartiest of bird hunters.

On the other hand, with deep, powdery snow for night roosting, grouse are in winter heaven. Their habit of roosting in the upper reaches of pines has suddenly been abandoned for more favorable snow roosts—a behavior that conserves energy and contributes to better over-winter survival.

When I was twenty-something, my buddies and I would put on our felted-lined, rubber-bottomed boots and wade through knee-deep snow.

Winter grouse hunting in Wisconsin may include deep snow, as Rocky, the author's family German shorthair, can attest to.

Subsequently, at thirty- and forty-something, I slowed down considerably but would occasionally strap on my snowshoes and head for the tag alder–edged swamps. At fifty-something, I was put to the test more than once. One weekend, a close friend and hunting buddy Dale and I trudged through the season's first snowfall, which, after a bit of rain, left about eight inches of wet, crusty snow. We managed a mile-and-a-half swing through the woods and in the process, Dale—much to both of our delights—put a brace of grouse in the bag.

Another outing with several good friends included snowshoes but eroded into a combination hunt and ice-fishing excursion. This annual end-of-the-year tradition typically involves hunts either an hour north and an hour south of our place. One year, we encountered snow up north but bare, November-like conditions to the south.

Three things I most love about this time of the year are late-season grouse hunting, old dogs and cold, finger-numbing winter days in the woods. I hope to spend a bit of time with all three once again. The dogs and I will explore the woods close to home, searching for wintering ruffed grouse. Together, we will hunt on paper mill land, state wildlife management areas and on property along the Wisconsin River bottoms.

Snowshoes will be in order, as the knee-deep snow can be a real chore for an aging hunter. During those hunts—if history repeats itself—I will take a couple of spills while traversing the cattail marshes along frozen backwater sloughs. Falling on snowshoes in deep snow is easy. Getting back up is another matter. Using my gun for support, after unloading, I'll get back on my feet and head for frozen backwater sloughs and beaver ponds. There, the snow isn't as deep and makes for easier going.

Grouse hunting after the snow gets deep is often a labor of love. And that's why hunting "old ruff" in January trips my trigger. It makes hunting grouse the following year in October that much more enjoyable.

Hunting with an old bird dog is just plain satisfying, and hours spent are quality time for sure. Each hunt could be the last, but here's always hope for just one more season together.

Finger-numbing days? Well, knowing there's a warm truck and home to go back to at the end of the day helps. And the long, cold winter gives us pause to dream about spring, summer and fall.

The author used snowshoes on a late-season hunt in north-central Wisconsin.

Gone are the golden days of autumn, as lush foliage has been replaced by snow, naked trees and chill arctic winds. Walking takes on new meaning when snow reaches the top of one's boots—no longer are hunts a casual stroll through the woods. Grouse have taken to sleeping in snow banks and feeding on the sly, early and late in the day. To do otherwise would likely prove fatal.

Most upland hunters have stored their shotguns, some long before the first snowflakes hit the ground. The few who persist have given up their light vests, jackets and rubber boots for heavy wool, fleece and hooded parkas. Long underwear and insulated boots are now the rule.

It has become a family tradition, our winter holiday ruffed grouse hunts. And ever since son Erik went out-of-state for a higher education, it has become a homecoming event of sorts. A regular holiday ritual, standing the test of time. This year is no exception.

On the first Monday, the boys, Erik and Karl, and I visited a cover we call the Railroad Crossing that borders a black spruce and tamarack bog. For

Rocky poses on the edge of a snow-covered grouse woods near the author's home in north-central Wisconsin.

some reason, grouse gather there in December, and since discovering their hideout, we pay them at least one visit each season. While working the bog's snow-covered alder edge, the boys and their dog named Sue moved five grouse, one of which fell to Erik's gun. A half-hour later, we checked a place labeled Six Mile, which yielded not a single flush but afforded another brisk walk in ankle-deep snow while our dogs Rocky and Sue enjoyed one more chance to stretch their legs.

On Tuesday, we visited a location closer to home by a neighbor's beaver pond, dubbed the Mother Cover. We worked its length, almost a quarter mile, without success. Not until we explored an adjacent cover bordering a picked cornfield did we see a single bird that offered no shot. Next on our agenda was an old standby near the Phantom Grouse Cover that failed to produce, so we called it a day. That evening, after adding a couple of previously harvested birds from the freezer, our family sat down to a delicious meal of grouse alfredo, prepared by Erik.

Wednesday morning dawned with an eastern red sky and the promise of another major snowstorm. After chores around the house, we snuck off to several other spots close at hand. But that was after I wrote this story, so all I can promise is a vision of what might have been.

With luck, after Christmas, the boys and I will connect with several close friends for another holiday habit, a New Year's grouse hunt in Lincoln, Wood or Monroe Counties with Tim, Rich and their boys.

As you can see, surrounding myself with family and friends in the woods is truly a holiday tradition.

What a difference a year can make. A year prior, during late-season ruffed grouse hunting, snow depths were knee deep. January ruffed grouse hunting was next to impossible. Some years, even December woods can be problematic.

But this year in December, late-season ruffed grouse hunting was a real possibility. In my home county of Portage, snow depths ranged from four inches at the northern county line and next to nothing at the southern border. No snow roosting for grouse, at least at that point. Grouse were roosting off the ground—utilizing the protection offered by dense pine trees. That's where son Erik and I took the dogs for our annual holiday hunt.

He was home for Christmas and bought a non-resident small game hunting license. You see, he lives out east where he teaches wildlife courses at the University of Maine in Orono. He flew home for a week—grading papers at our kitchen table in the evening, spending daylight hours visiting relatives. And on several occasions, he hunted pheasants and grouse with his old man.

It's an annual holiday affair. Five years ago, we found a spot on the Paul Olson Wildlife Area near Rudolph that attracted pheasants. We have yet to kill one there, but they have provided us exercise and always give Buster a good go. One year, a large rooster offered my son a shot but escaped without losing a feather. Another year, all we found was a pair of fresh tracks in the snow.

One weekend, we switched gears and concentrated on grouse. Saturday, we hunted the Mead State Wildlife Area north of Milladore. Fresh tracks in the snow in aspen clear-cuts and along alder swales led us to a single flush on the edge of a spruce bog. "That's right where Buster flushed one

The author's son Erik displaying his holiday hunt prize—a large male ruffed grouse.

last year," Erik remarked. "It snuck out on the opposite side of the alders. I didn't have a chance for a shot."

Sunday was his last full day home, and with the Packer game scheduled that afternoon, we headed back to the spruce bog in the morning. Erik declared, "I'm going to take the dog in from the opposite direction and try to outsmart that bird." With that, he unloaded his brother's German shorthaired pointer Finn from a dog box, loaded his gun and headed for the spruces.

I took Buster into a nearby mature pine plantation that bordered an alder swale—an area that in years past produced several grouse flushes. Despite giving it his all, he failed to find a single bird. I returned to the truck, loaded Buster in a dog box and drove a half mile down the road to where we had agreed to meet. While exiting the truck and stepping on the road, I heard a single shot one hundred yards into the woods.

Erik and Finn emerged from the woods and displayed their prize—a large male ruffed grouse—capping off a perfect ending to that year's annual holiday hunt.

21
Closing Days

We stood on hallowed ground that closing day and held a bird in our hands—within 100 yards of the exact spot my Tina dog blessed me with a lifetime memory.

I could have just waved goodbye. But Buster, my sidekick field-bred English cocker spaniel, and I felt the urge to get outside in the grouse woods one more time. You see, the season to hunt ruffed grouse with a gun ends the last day of January in Wisconsin. The final week of this year's hunt was a real weather roller-coaster. Schools were closed Monday and Tuesday due to extreme wind-chill warnings—minus-sixty-five below zero. Wednesday, it had "moderated" to minus ten below zero without the wind chill. When it warmed up to plus twenty degrees on Thursday, we were ready to go but woke up to a snowstorm that left another five inches. Visibility was terrible, so we waited until Friday, closing day. Just as well, as there's a special place in my heart for closing day.

Hunting the Mead Wildlife Area, just northwest of our place, has been an end of the season tradition as long as I can remember. When I wore a younger man's boots, the last day of grouse season meant snowshoes and deep treks into interior portions of the thirty-three-thousand-acre state wildlife area. In doing so, my dogs would mostly find and point birds where tag alder met cattails along the fringes of frozen flowages.

This year, Buster and I were rewarded with blue skies, a fresh blanket of cotton-white snow and no wind to speak of. The truck thermometer read three degrees above zero as we pulled out of the driveway and once again headed to the Mead, six miles down the road.

We did our annual Mead "drive about." Curiosity gets the better of me. I want to see if there are any other hunters out on the last day. There are seven main roads that border and bisect the Mead. Many dead-end roads stab the interior and end at parking lots. Except for one or two, the lots and dead ends were all but snowbound. So, my survey was complete as I traversed the property that touches the borders of Portage, Marathon and Wood Counties.

Not counting activity at the property's main office and education center, I observed only two parked vehicles. One, looking like a family SUV, was in a plowed parking lot—a trailhead to a plowed logging road on the east end. The other, a trapper's Jeep, was parked on the edge of the southern bordering county highway. The well-worn snowshoe trail from his vehicle and along a drainage ditch to the north told his story.

Buster and I chose to park not far from Smokey Hill—where French troops and Chippewas defeated the Ho-Chunks in a fierce battle back in 1748. Loggers were active and provided a plowed road and access to a large aspen stand. It was a location son Erik and I visited and found grouse over the Christmas holiday.

Anyway, as I suspected, this time around, the snow was twenty-seven inches deep in the woods—perfect conditions for snow-roosting grouse. Buster had a blast. He hit the snow searching for grouse with the same reckless abandon as he does fetching a duck from a pond in fall. In both cases, it involved swimming. For the most part, I stuck to the plowed logging road. Walking in snow over ones' knees is not for old-timers and the faint of heart.

No grouse were seen or heard. But in the final analysis, we kept alive our closing day tradition. I had a good walk in the frigid winter woods, and my Buster boy had a blast, doing exactly what he was born to do.

Isn't that what it's all about?

The forecast was for another three to five inches of snow. In the woods, there was nearly a foot of old, crusty snow. The grouse season ended on a Tuesday, and I still had the urge to hunt. Not many grouse hunt this time of the year, but by tradition, I always find time for an annual season-ending hunt. By the time Buster and I hit the woods—following a trail plowed in by loggers earlier in the month—snow was coming down hard. The temperature was fourteen degrees Fahrenheit. We flushed no birds. We spotted nary a track in the snow.

The Mead state wildlife area, just down the road, is a perfect location to cure our need for just one last hunt. I have no illusions. Late-season grouse hunting is not easy. Unlike glorious walks through colorful October woods, looking for grouse in the dead of winter is difficult, to say the least. I recall hunting on snowshoes in my younger years—the only way to go when snow depths were knee-deep. These days, it's more a labor of love than productive. Looking back at forty-eight years of grouse hunting, I remember only shooting a few during late season.

Back at the truck and off the side of the main road, we spotted a budding grouse in an aspen. The gun was already cased in the truck, and I had no urge to kill the last bird I'd see this season. Call it superstition, call it a bad luck omen. So, instead, I grabbed my phone and digitally bagged him. Yes, it was a male. Got close enough to see his tail feathers. Close enough to take a picture.

I watched him rocket off to a spot I know well. In four months, I will listen for his drumming. RGS biologists explain, male grouse

> *are aggressively territorial throughout their adult lives, defending for their almost exclusive use a piece of woodland that is 6–10 acres in extent. Usually this is shared with one or two hens. The male grouse proclaims his property rights by engaging in a "drumming" display. This sound is made by beating his wings against the air to create a vacuum, as lightning does when it makes thunder. The drummer usually stands on a log, stone or mound of dirt when drumming, and this object is called a "drumming log." He does not strike the log to make the noise, he only uses the "drumming log" as a stage for his display.*
>
> *The drumming stage selected by a male is most likely to be about 10–12 inches above the ground, in moderately dense brush, (usually 70 to 160 stems within a 10-ft. radius) where he can maintain unrestricted surveillance over the terrain for a radius of about 60 ft. Across much of the Ruffed Grouse range there are usually mature male aspens within sight in the forest canopy overhead. Drumming occurs throughout the year, so long as his "log" is not too deeply buried under snow. In the spring, drumming becomes more frequent and prolonged as the cock grouse advertises his location to hens seeking a mate.*

A budding male grouse posed for the author on a closing-day winter hunt.

And as far as my winter grouse goes, I'll return to his home range to look for his drumming log come April. And hopefully he'll kindly pose for another picture.

Friend Phred killed this grouse. At the very least he inspired the deed. After sharing the story of his redemption hunt in Kansas and my feeling of guilt for not going out grouse hunting at least one more time, son Karl and I took his pup Sage out one last time yesterday—closing out the season.

We found a spot close to home that had some logging activity in progress, allowing these old legs access to a spot dear to my heart. I consider this area hallowed ground, as it is a cover that presented me with my one and only true double on grouse—thirty years ago.

I was hunting a father-and-daughter pair of shorthairs, Buck and Tina, on public land during December and a high in the cycle. Most of the hunt's

Most years, hunting dogs and hunters encounter deep snow on closing-day hunts for ruffed grouse.

details are fuzzy, but I remember the moment Tina's bell stopped, the instant I reacted to the multiple flush and the length of time I held the pair of birds in my hands. It's a memory burned permanently in my mind. In addition, I can take you to the exact spot Tina and I shared that day.

And that is exactly where Karl and I ended this time around. Sage found a grouse hiding in a clump of alders. The bird tumbled as we shot simultaneously. Perfect, I thought, now we can both close the door on this year's hunt on a high note.

Son Erik later called for an autopsy—as I shoot a 28-gauge with no. 6 bismuth, Karl shoots a 20-gauge with no. 8 lead. I said no. I did not want to break the magic spell that transpired—as father, son and pup were closer than we have been in a long time.

We stood on hallowed ground that closing day and held a bird in our hands, within one hundred yards of the exact spot my Tina dog blessed me with a lifetime memory.

Sometimes you can go back…

It was a trip down memory lane. The last day of the ruffed grouse season and I returned to where it all began—forty-two years ago.

Just west of our place along the creek lies thirty-three thousand acres of public land locally referred to as "The Mead." Property boundary signs appear five miles from our driveway. Stretching ten miles east and west by four miles north and south, the Mead's forty square miles of flowages, wetlands, upland forests and grasslands is a hunter's and nature lover's paradise indeed.

Buster, my field-bred English cocker sidekick, and I loaded up the truck for one last grouse hunt. We drove west from home and headed to places we know so well. Along the way, we chased dreams of tomorrow and pleasant memories from the past.

County Highway O took us north past the spot I hunted grouse and woodcock with several friends more than four decades ago—a place where friend Dale's Brittany Jesse pointed and retrieved her first woodcock—past a trail named after a black bear spotted by a friend while motorcycling to a nearby hunting dog field trial. Then we drove past the dog training field trial area that friend Mike, Mead project manager Tom Meier and I worked together to establish back in the early 1980s. For nearly two decades, we hosted a statewide woodcock and grouse field trial fundraiser along the Little Eau Pleine River bottoms.

We slipped over the county line into Marathon and followed County Highway C west to a place Buster flushed and retrieved his first grouse four years earlier. It's an area that is heavily managed for young forest wildlife, and it was near there we parked the truck for a short one-hour hunt. The snow was deep enough to accommodate open snowmobile trails and an energetic cocker spaniel. Grouse tracks said birds were in the neighborhood, but alas, none revealed themselves to us that day.

Farther down the road, we passed a special stone fence covert where son Erik shot two grouse several years apart. Then our journey turned south along County Highway S. Past Teal Flowage, where both of my sons learned to hunt ducks during early season youth hunts. Past an open field where then project manager John Berkhahn hosted the very first public dog training seminar with field trail association members—and my puppy Dusty stole the show during an introduction to birds demonstration. We traveled past a dead-end road leading to the Honey Island flowage, where I shot my first limit of woodcock over my first bird dog named Buck back in 1975.

Across the road, the Mead Education and Visitor Center stood out prominently against the snow-white landscape. A far cry from the old, original metal project office, it stands tall—a new chapter and a testament to forward thinkers and outdoor educators. Under the new building's shadow, I recall a woodcock son Karl and I banded one spring, a bear friend Tim's dog pointed in a den in adjacent alder cover and a grouse son Erik and I both missed on the fringe of nearby Little Birch Flowage.

West again on County Highway H brought us to Smokey Hill Road, where the boss and I have conducted spring woodcock singing ground surveys for the U.S. Fish and Wildlife Service for nearly three decades. Son Karl passed up a sure shot at a grouse perched in a tree—showing his old man that even as a young man, his personal ethics ran deep. Then crossing Countyline Road, I recalled a duck hunt thirty-four years ago—the day after meeting my future wife on a blind date. I remember killing a teal, the dog's retrieve and asking friend Dale—who set up the date—if he knew her phone number.

We passed the foot of Smokey Hill, where legend has it a Chippewa tribe camped and, with the help of French soldiers, fought off marauding Winnebago tribesmen. Today, a flowage at the base of the hill serves as waterfowl refuge. Not far from there and across the Little Eau Pleine River is a spot where forty years ago Professor Nauman handed me a clipboard, then grabbed his shotgun and joined hundreds of opening weekend duck hunters on North Smokey Hill Flowage. Fellow student and friend Ron and I were left to check hunter bags as they came off the flowage.

Ah, memories. So many pleasant memories from the Mead. So many, I could write a book. Maybe someday I will.

22
A Bird Dog for Baby Spraefke

No one can fully understand the meaning of love unless he's owned a dog. A dog can show you more honest affection with a flick of his tail than a man can gather through a lifetime of handshakes.
—Gene Hill, "The Dog Man," Tears and Laughter, *1981*

There is a special place tucked in the north woods, nestled in aspen and alders, where a country church once stood with pride. It burned to the ground in 1948, and today, all that indicates its existence are a pair of white crosses—the smaller of the two marking a single grave site of an unnamed newborn that died in 1937. Not long ago, the setting took on new meaning. And that story, as told by bird dog club member Rich, includes an English pointer named Ranger.

"Legend has it that the child in the grave is a daughter of William Spraefke, a.k.a. Whiskey Bill. Not sure if that is true, but the road near the grave was once named Whiskey Bill Road and has since been renamed Spraefke Road. I know there was a man named William Spraefke that lived in the woods off that road at that time. So, it all makes some sense." And according to Rich, "The two crosses are about thirty yards north of Whiskey Bill Road and are nestled in mature aspen with an understory of some alder, a thorn apple thicket and some scattered balsam. You really can't see any remnants of the church or foundation."

Fourteen years ago, Rich and his family packed their truck and experienced 140 miles of "white knuckle driving" through "a January blizzard that we had no business going out in" to pick up an eight-week-old pointer puppy of English decent. They made it home safe and sound and welcomed "a friend and companion that enriched the lives of our family." But the thing that intrigued Rich the most was "the way he looked into my eyes—literally for hours and hours over his lifetime. What was he thinking?"

Ranger was well traveled—including multiple trips to Montana, North and South Dakota and, of course, throughout Wisconsin. Rich recalls many highlights—fourteen years of memories. Like in North Dakota, during his first fall and witnessed by friends, including yours truly, "When my pride and joy ran over a big hill and disappeared chasing a large white-tailed buck." And 1998–2000 were "three years of the best ruffed grouse hunting I've ever had—with the dog that all three sons shot their first birds over. He was in the prime of his life." Or later, the time he became lost pheasant hunting in South Dakota for forty-five minutes and "we found him on point—pointing a rooster near the exact spot we last saw him."

One past fall in Montana, during the twilight of Ranger's life, "the old boy nailed a covey of Hungarian partridge at the end of a shelterbelt on an abandoned homestead and then proceeded to find singles for me and the rest of our party."

On his last night, he slept with Rich's eighteen-year-old son Corey, a young man who left for the Marines the following spring. "Bulletproof and full of macho, sleeping on the floor with an old bird dog, no doubt sharing memories, smiles and tears."

Rich buried Ranger near Whiskey Bill's infant daughter. "So, in my mind, I have taken him where there are plenty of grouse and have given the best bird dog I've ever owned to a child that never had a dog."

Rest in peace, buddy.

23
WOODCOCK HEAVEN

Cloaked in dogwood, willow, alder and aspen—somewhat jungle-like—it's a place only woodcock, worms and woodcock hunters and their dogs dare tread.

There's a special place in heaven for woodcock hunters. With any luck, there's a spot reserved there for me. If not, I'd like to get on the waiting list. In the meantime, I know a place on earth just like it—a little slice of heaven, don't you know.

Cloaked in dogwood, willow, alder and aspen—somewhat jungle-like—it's a place only woodcock, worms and woodcock hunters and their dogs dare tread. Sprinkle in a dash of briars, nettles and goldenrod along the edges and open grasslands between islands of aspen, and the ingredients for a woodcock lodge have been assembled.

Moisture is another key component. During times of drought, the covert will be empty. Water pushes worms toward the surface. Then a woodcock's two-and-a-half-inch bill can probe, grab and swallow its prey like spaghetti noodles. Local and migrant birds alike need worms—lots of worms—to build up fat reserves for the fall flight south. Woodcock from southern Canada and the Upper Midwest must retreat down the Mississippi River valley to southern states like Louisiana—where the ground and worms never freeze.

So, that special place is where son Karl and our dogs traveled for the opening of the woodcock hunting season. Southern Portage County was our destination, where we met up with friends Mike, Marty and Glen.

A woodcock engraved on the author's brass dog whistle depicts one of his favorite game birds.

A place we've dubbed "Woodcock Heaven"—an extraordinary location known to us for more than forty years. Bird dog club member and close friend Mike liked it so much that he bought it several years ago, and it's there he plans to retire. His stewardship of the land over the past few decades has insured abundant woodcock for his children and grandchildren in the future. You see, woodcock are young forest game birds and share their home with a host of other resident songbirds, small animals, amphibians, insects and worms. Rotational clear-cutting of aspen and alder does the trick. Stimulation of dogwood and willow are just two of the many beneficial results of clear-cutting.

We hunted during the coolest part of the day, and our bird dogs found woodcock. Not in the numbers we'd find the next month, when migrant birds from up north arrive, but enough for a couple of meals. Prepared correctly and cooked on the grill, woodcock is a gourmet's delight.

Buster loves woodcock. He flushed his fair share over the weekend. And his master managed to bag a pair of birds. After all, he's a cocker spaniel, and I'm a mediocre shot. His ancestors from England were made to order for woodcock hunting—thus the name "cocker" spaniel. Trained to flush European woodcock within range of their hunter's shotgun, they hunt close and with vigor. To this day, the queen of England harbors cocker spaniels in her family's Royal Kennels.

While savoring our weekend hunt, we were serenaded by bird-hunting cowboys and cowgirls following and singing to their pointers and setters. They rode horses across the adjacent grasslands while field trialing their bird dogs—using blank guns and monitoring the resident prairie chicken populations. It's a tradition as old as the state-owned grassland property and one we look forward to viewing every September.

While the sun set in the west, we rested on Mike's retirement home's deck. There we ate grilled woodcock and sipped beer. We also listened to honking geese and trumpeting cranes as they joined the cowboy concert.

A slice of heaven indeed.

24
Pheasant Hunting

Throughout much of their range, pheasants are found in close company with other upland birds. In fact, some hunters seek situations where they are going to be surprised by what materializes when they step in front of their pointing dog, or by what their retriever or spaniel flushes from the brush.
—*Larry Brown, "A Mixed Bag,"* A Pheasant Hunter's Notebook

I remember hunting wild pheasants opening weekends in Eau Claire County in the 1980s with two college friends, Dan and Mike. We had access to private land and did rather well. And like author Larry Brown, we were blessed with mixed bags of pheasant, quail and ruffed grouse. The hill country of western and southwestern Wisconsin was like that back then and may be the same in pockets of good habitat to this day.

Coveys of bobwhites along brushy fence rows, pheasants in cattail swales and grassy buffers along cultivated fields and grouse scattered in woodlots on steep hillsides. Weekends in October with Dan and his Labrador retrievers still resonate in my memory bank.

A few years ago, I traveled downstream in December to gather food for thought and the table. A brown-bag lunch seminar on hunting ethics at the Aldo Leopold Foundation's Leopold Center near Baraboo in Sauk County provided something to ponder. And earlier that morning, a pheasant hunt with my gun dog Buster offered some game for the table.

What better prelude to a lecture on hunting ethics than a late-season hunt in the land of Leopold? That's exactly what Buster and I did at a nearby state wildlife area named Pine Island, a 5,499-acre property located just west of Portage, which according to the DNR consists of approximately 1,200 acres of wetland habitat, 1,000 acres of grassland, 1,500 acres of oak/savanna habitat and 1,900 acres of wooded habitat. The property lies in the floodplains of the Wisconsin and Baraboo Rivers and includes several islands of the Wisconsin River.

Rumor had it the state was stocking many public hunting areas with mature rooster pheasants right up to season's end, the last day of December. We hunted one area that spanned hundreds of acres of grassland. There, only a single set of tracks appeared, showing their age under a fresh layer of snow. That was not the case at another location across the rather enormous property. Buster was immediately on the trail of several birds that called an unharvested sunflower field home. He flushed a pair of roosters from a small aspen thicket adjacent to the sunflowers. The first flew out of range, and the other one ran past me at twenty yards, but by the time it was fair game and airborne, several large trees blocked my vision.

We followed up on the first bird. Buster quickly found him and another in a row of windbreak pines. One presented me with possible shot, but I held back rather than shoot toward a road and a passing truck. Soon after that, I spotted yet another rooster crossing a harvested cornfield, but it disappeared in adjacent marsh grass. When we crossed his tracks in the field, I sent Buster in on the hot trail. It led him into two brush piles near an old barn foundation. The boisterous rooster cackled as it exploded from the second snow-covered pile and flew by me right to left.

Buster made short order of a forty-yard retrieve to my side. I admired the beautifully colored, long-tailed bird for a moment, then thanked my dog and looked at the clock. If we hurried, we'd make the noon seminar.

The speaker on the afternoon agenda was Dr. Christopher R. Webster, professor of quantitative ecology at the Michigan Technological University. He discussed the evolving role of hunters in the conservation and management of wild ungulate populations, the changing landscape of deer abundance, ecological impacts and the contemporary role of hunting in Aldo Leopold's view of a land ethic.

Whoa! That's a mouthful for this old rough-shooting hunter to swallow. But let me attempt a translated summary for those of us with little more than a license to hunt and gather. The professor detailed Leopold's belief in the cultural value of hunting, likewise the "sports, customs and experiences that renew contacts with wild things." According to Leopold, those cultural values number three.

Wisconsin is blessed with ample opportunities to bag pheasants like these in suitable habitat.

First, a hereditary fever to hunt afflicts many in any given population. He felt "hunting reminds us of our distinctive national origins and evolution—such awareness is 'nationalism' in its best sense." He dubbed it the "split-rail" value—a Daniel Boone, fur trade romance.

The second value of the hunting experience is that it reminds us of the soil-plant-animal-man food chain. As one seminar participant put it, "Yes. I recall very well the animals I kill and eat. But I'll never know the cows that give their lives to give me a hamburger."

And the third of Leopold's values is the ethical restraints or codes that hunters develop over time—"collectively called sportsmanship…as the hunter ordinarily has no gallery to applaud or disapprove of his conduct. Whatever his acts, they are dictated by his own conscience, rather than by a mob of onlookers. It is difficult to exaggerate the importance of this fact."

Our speaker also dipped his toe into the hunters' role in deer management and abundance—an issue that spans all the way back to the 1940s, when deer populations exploded in the north and thrust Leopold deep into Wisconsin's first controversial doe hunt.

My trip downstream that early winter weekday was well worth the time and gas. And Buster was one happy hunter. He now knows well his role in the food chain.

25
BUSTER

Buster hit the ground running right off the bat and, despite my faults as a trainer, bucked the establishment and has performed at a high level in the field from early on.

He was born in June 2010. I found him among a litter of eight-week-old puppies at Fallen Wings Kennels near Hilbert in Calumet County. There, two of the top breeders in the nation, Rumi and Mike Schroeder, introduced me to the wonderful world of field-bred English cocker spaniels.

At two months old, he entered our lives and soon became the center of attention among a kennel full of hunting dogs. By the time he reached twelve months, he stood eighteen and a half inches tall at the shoulders and weighed thirty-seven pounds—the top end of his breed's standards. Despite his stature, he was, at the time, the smallest dog among our much larger German shorthaired pointers—nearly twice his size. But his proportions did not deter his personality and ego. In his own mind, Buster was the official kennel boss.

The breed club also notes they are "merry and affectionate, of equable disposition, neither sluggish nor hyperactive, a willing worker and a faithful and engaging companion." An understatement, I might add. Most who hunt over the breed will note "they will make you laugh." Buster is all of that—merry, affectionate and bold in the woods, field and marshes.

Faithful readers of my weekly outdoor newspaper column watched Buster mature over the years. He turned eight this past summer. They read about

Buster, the author's English cocker spaniel, proudly poses with a woodcock he flushed and retrieved.

his travels with me to the Canadian prairies of Saskatchewan, northwest to North Dakota and Montana, to the marshes and cornfields of Iowa and, of course, throughout Wisconsin. Together, we've put some miles behind us to get to this point.

Conventional wisdom has long declared that gun dogs reach their prime between ages six through ten. Buster hit the ground running right off the bat and, despite my faults as a trainer, bucked the establishment and has performed at a high level in the field from early on. He is a flushing dog that hunts for the gun, seldom ranges out of range and quarters the woods and fields in search of his quarry like a pro. Made retrieves that took my breath away. Found wounded game birds and waterfowl other dogs would have given up on. Flushed countless woodcock, grouse, pheasant and prairie game birds like Huns and sharp-tails. Now, he is, no doubt, at the top of his game.

The purchase of Buster back in 2010 was not a fluke. He was, and still is, a dream of mine that dates to my teenage years. Back in the 1970s, I chanced on a hunter and his two cocker spaniels hunting woodcock in southern Wisconsin. Multiple gunshots drew my attention to an alder swale at the headwaters of a small stream bisecting a public hunting grounds named Karcher Marsh near Burlington. The hunter was kind enough to introduce this dogless hunter to his cockers. It took nearly forty years of pointing German dogs, but I ultimately found my cockers in Buster and subsequently unrelated sisters from Ohio—namely Bingo and Belle. Those three have since produced several beautiful litters of puppies for our kennel, merry and affectionate gun dogs that have found hunting homes in seven other states and, of course, Wisconsin.

Buster has been and will continue to be my sidekick. I share our adventures where ever they may take us—for as long as we're together and eventually past both our primes.

26
ON THE TAIL OF A STORM

The hike spurred memories from the past. Passing graves of dogs from days gone by will do just that.

It happened after one of several summer storm fronts blew across the river valley and the tornado warnings had expired. We found ourselves on the kennel porch, sipping refreshing drinks and enjoying the cool breeze that followed the storm pushing the hot, humid weather east.

While watching young Jordan, working his cocker spaniels in the prairie grass field east of the kennel, the boss commented, "He reminds me of you at that age."

"What do you mean?" I asked. "Good looking, fit and trim, well-trained dogs?"

"No, obsessed—and training dogs on his wedding anniversary no less. I want to meet his wife and warn her."

"Hey. I only forgot our anniversary twice in thirty years."

"You mean, two times in thirty-one years—and what about my birthday? How many times on that account? Hmmm?"

"Here we go," I lamented. "Can we change the subject?"

Silence—my favorite subject. A few minutes later, Buster, our English cocker, jumped up on my lap and pointed his nose into the wind.

"What do you smell, buddy? Could fall be in the air? Or are you smelling Jordan's little girl Polly?

He looked up at me with more questions than answers in his eyes and whined. That translated into, "Can I go out in the field? Go swimming in the pond? Retrieve the training dummy a couple hundred times? Can I? Can I? Can I?"

"Let's go for a walk," chirped the boss.

We followed the mowed trail that led to the pond. There we entertained Buster for a spell with a retrieving dummy and walk around the pond. As I recall, the hike spurred memories from the past. Passing graves of dogs from days gone by will do just that.

On the high banks of our creek, the bones of my first bird dog lie in a grave. A German shorthaired pointer, Buck found his way into my heart back in 1974. He lived in my dorm room at the local state college for a while—until we were both asked to move off-campus. I learned from Buck much of what I now know not to do when training a gun dog. He lived a couple months shy of sixteen years. Not far from his grave lies Maddie. Owned and trained by son Karl, I recalled the day we buried her and the

Dakota, one of the author's favorite German shorthairs, is buried in a special spot under a willow tree by the training pond.

simple, poignant words from a fourteen-year-old boy in her memory, "She was a good dog." Around the corner, along several rows of pines, lie Duke, Kane, Buck Junior, Little Bucky, Tucker, Mac and Jack. The trail led back to a pond in the training field where Dakota and Rocky rest under a weeping willow tree. Near the pond, a pair wolf trees left by the previous landowner, farmer Fred, marks a long list of female shorthairs—Tina, Dusty, Shana, Coco, Munch, Cody, Bingo, Molly, Becky II, Suzy, Mossy, Jerzy, Mossy II and Becky III. Somewhere else on trails cutting through our forty acres are the final resting points for Cash, Pokey and Spook—three shorthairs that called son Erik their very own. And finally, along the trail leading away from the pond is a small wooden cross marking Little Rock's stone-covered grave—a constant reminder that sometimes, good dogs die young.

Buster worked the cover along the edges of the trail like he was on a mission. But then again, he's a cocker and that's their life calling—finding and flushing birds for their master. But by the willow tree, he paused to mark his territory on Dakota's grave. "Now, how did he know Dakota was one of my favorites?" I thought.

On the tail of a storm that day we reminisced, took a stroll down memory lane and returned to the kennel, where the next generations of German pointers and English cockers waited in their runs. A litter of pups in the whelping room had just opened their eyes and were intent on their mother's care. The outside kennel runs needed cleaning, and it was time for the dogs to be fed once again.

27
DEAR DR. DEAN

Come October, our boarding kennel will be closed and the dogs and I will be "working out" daily. Where this hunter's road leads in October remains to be seen. November will bring the nine-day deer season, December and January late season ruffed grouse hunting. My blood pressure is beginning to drop just thinking about it.

Dear Dr. Dean,

I realize this report on my health is a bit premature, but I had an inspiration to drop you a note just the same—so as not to bore you with all the following details during my regularly scheduled checkup. Let's consider this a rehash of the state of my annual health address, albeit an unofficial, nonclinical analysis.

As a sportsman in your own right, you of all people should know the medicinal value of participating in outdoor sports. Now that fall is upon us, I honestly hope you play hooky from the clinic on occasion and secretly toss a fly or two for trout, or musky—hunting for yet another elusive fifty-incher before the water turns to ice. After all, it was the famous outdoor humorist Ed Zern who said, "Fishing is a pursuit calculated to promote longevity," and convinced his wife—who knew he carried little life insurance—"he ought to go fishing instead of staying home putting up the screens, or taking them down, or just hanging around and carrying out the garbage once and a while."

One of the author's German shorthairs waits patiently for his turn to exercise his master.

In my case, the urge to follow bird dogs in October begins in early September. Son Karl and I will travel west to the Tomah area next week for the ruffed grouse opener. Despite midday heat, abundant ticks, mosquitoes and heavy foliage, the dogs will enjoy the cool, early-morning temperatures and dew on the grasses and ferns. We will notice an increase in grouse numbers, as the population cycle is on the rise. Woodcock will be abundant in the lowlands, gorging on earthworms as they build fat reserves for October's southerly migration urges. They'll have nothing to fear from us, as the season to hunt woodcock doesn't open until September 23. With luck on our side, we'll have a couple of grouse in our game bags at the end of the day. If not, we'll be sweating, leg weary and exactly where we want to be. And a bit healthier and happier for the effort.

So, beginning this month, a regular dose of exercise—cardiovascular in nature—is on my agenda. Come October, our boarding kennel will be closed, and the dogs and I will be "working out" daily. Where this hunter's road leads in October remains to be seen. November will bring the nine-day deer season, December and January late ruffed grouse hunting. My blood pressure is beginning to drop just thinking about it. All other vital signs appear stable. I lost ten pounds in August by giving up breadstuff and beer—except for the occasional brew celebrating my weight-loss success. My appetite is fine, yet I should lose a pound or two each week along the way. By the end of the season, I should be fit as a fiddle.

Author Havilah Babcock, in his book, *My Health Is Better in November*, described a hunter's overall well-being as follows: "Outdoor pursuits have a therapeutic value, a stirring day in the field purges the mind. When the first frost comes, there is a noticeable improvement in his health."

So, by the time I see you later this week, I ought to pass your examination with flying colors. Better yet, why don't we just postpone my appointment a few months? By mid-January, I should be done grouse hunting and in pretty good shape—for the shape I'm in.

Yours in good health, Ken

28

MACQUARRIE LOVED PA'TRIDGE HUNTING

MacQuarrie brought the outdoors to the library literature, and he brought the library to the outdoors. He did it with a magnificent idiom, a flashing wit and the wry wisdom that remembers the impermanence of man's mightiest edifices. [He] established the modern school of outdoor writing and it is not too much to say that if Aldo Leopold cut a path for man to follow in making terms with his environment, MacQuarrie lighted it to show the way.
—Dion Henderson, MacQuarrie obituary, 1956

Grandpa Ivan loved to fish. He craved musky fishing—so much so that he'd tie his canoe to the top of his 1930 Buick, load gear and supplies for a week and head north from the city—enduring a laborious, day-long trip to Horsehead Lake near Presque Isle. "The roads weren't so good back then," said my mother. "I remember having to stop several times along the way to repair flat tires." That was around 1936, when mom was about fourteen years old. She fondly recalled trips up north with her father. "The men would fish all day, and my girlfriend and I would tend the cabin, play outside and cook. Dad would take us fishing for bluegills. That was a lot of fun too. There were only a couple of cabins on the lake then, it was a real wilderness."

Around the same time, a thirty-six-year-old newspaper man, Gordon MacQuarrie, became the outdoor editor of the *Milwaukee Journal*. Born in Superior, Wisconsin, he moved to Milwaukee to become the first full-time, professional outdoor writer in America. From his apartment in the city, he traveled the state and the country to share his weekly hunting and fishing outdoor adventures with huge numbers of loyal readers. His Old Duck Hunters' Association tales and trips to fish, hunt ducks and partridge across the state have become legendary. And travel he did.

"It was a bad night for driving north and west through Wisconsin," he wrote in a piece he called "Canvasback Comeback."

> *Beyond the windshield, through stabbing sleet and snow, the President of the Old Duck Hunters' Association waited. So, I kept a-going....Near Loretta-Draper, Wisconsin, I stopped at Flambeau Louie Johnson's and in twenty minutes consumed a warm meal, promised Edie Johnson on my honor I'd take it slow and easy....[T]he car surged up the hill into the storm, heading for Highway 70, the fire lane, Clam Lake, Cable, Drummond—and the Middle Eau Claire Lake of Bayfield County, where Hizzoner smoked and dozed and waited.*

Roads, back in those days, were nothing compared to today's mostly paved and graded infrastructure. Mom remembered surfaced roads giving way to gravel, dirt and logging roads north of Wausau. MacQuarrie further explained, "The fire lane straight north from Loretta-Draper is no playground for a hard-road driver. It demands a man of the Model T vintage....[B]ig trees went down in that night's wind....[T]wice I got out and whaled away with an ax to clear the road."

Today's roads are an outdoor enthusiast's dream compared to my grandpa's generation. What took him, my mother and MacQuarrie all day can be accomplished these days in mere hours. A while back, I traced MacQuarrie's path—in short order, by the way—to Bayfield County and the town of Barnes, home of the Barnes Area Historical Museum. My pilgrimage followed Loretta-Draper on Highway 70, the fire lane (now a county highway), Clam Lake, Cable, Drummond—and the Middle Eau Claire Lake of Bayfield County. 218 miles. No flat tires, no trees on the roads. And in just under four hours.

Gordon MacQuarrie was a duck hunter, but he loved hunting ruffed grouse. He savored walking through Wisconsin's October north woods. In his piece

"Nothing to Do for Three Weeks," he wrote, "It was the best time, the beginning of the last week in October. In the partridge woods I would pluck at the sleeve of reluctant Indian summer.…I thought how fine it would be if, throughout the year, the season would hang on dead center, as it often does in Wisconsin in late October and early November."

He hunted ruffed grouse, or as he clearly stated in his classic story "Pa'tridge Fever—Cause and Cure," "No badger hillbilly would waste time wrapping his tongue around 'ruffed grouse.' And if you said 'Bonasa umbellus,' your man of the pa'tridge woods, from the Baraboo hills 300 miles north to Lake Superior's shore, would think you were swearing at him."

His "north of Wisconsin, in a warm, mellow world of gold and yellow and brown and red," lured him to places like the "'Cathedral'…a grove of stately Norway pines growing in a natural amphitheater perhaps a mile from the cabin." The cabin was headquarters for the Old Duck Hunters Association Inc., made famous by MacQuarrie in stories published in his outdoor newspaper column. It was from there on the shores of Middle Eau Claire Lake in southern Bayfield County that he and his father-in-law, Allan Peck "Hizzoner," hunted and fished extensively—the Cathedral being a favorite spot to hunt partridge.

"There is a feeling of reverence in your proper hunting man in such a place. Reverence, and if he had been there before, vigilant alertness, for you never know when the brown one with the fantail will explode from the forest floor and go slanting off among the big boles."

My good friend Wisconsin outdoor writer and photographer Keith Crowley wrote a full-length biography of MacQuarrie: *Gordon MacQuarrie: The Story of an Old Duck Hunter*. It is a must-read for fans of this literary legend. Keith takes us on MacQuarrie's life journey—from boyhood to an untimely death at age fifty-six. Keith ended the book believing Mac wrote his own epitaph when he penned the words, "He always shot them on the wing, never took more than his share, and loved the sport for its own sake."

In July 2017, the Barnes Area Historical Museum held a special event in MacQuarrie's honor. There, Keith talked about and showcased a special exhibit of Mac's memorabilia. Close to ninety fans of this nationally acclaimed writer joined me and invaded this small northern Wisconsin

A hunter explores MacQuarrie's north woods during the best of times in October.

community. Shortly thereafter, I became a charter member of the exclusive Old Duck Hunters Association Circle and, hope in doing so, helped to keep alive the memory of this great man and devoted pa'tridge hunter.

29
HUNTING THE FRINGES

The Wolf River in May or a blue October day still regularly pull me awash or afield, with a Springer spaniel for choice. I tend to seek the edges, the meeting place of plowed land and woods, in crisp weather. I learned my hunting from good men, farmers who did their own butchering and saw hunting as an extension of it. Few of us have such roots now, and hunting will perhaps eventually disappear. When it does, I hope to have disappeared too, but not before having done a bit to preserve its memory.
—Richard Yatzeck, Hunting the Edges, *1999*

Bird dog club member Phred brought author Richard Yatzeck to my attention years ago over drinks at his grouse camp located somewhere east of MacQuarrie's Libby Bay. Yatzeck, a professor of Russian literature at Lawrence University, apparently led student Phred astray with tales of grouse hunting and Russian prose. Phred lent me his copy of *Hunting the Edges*, which to this day, I have failed to return.

A chapter toward the end with the same title as the book caught my attention. While hunting the edges, the author and his longtime friend sought ruffed grouse at a place they both knew well twenty-four years previous. Hunting slow, they blundered into a flight of migrating woodcock, and their dogs presented them with rare limits of woodcock. Then, despite both "fledgling geezers" being as deaf as one of their aging bird dogs, they repeated twenty-year-old stories that were "sprouting gray whiskers" on the trail home. Aging hunters hunting the edges and reminiscing.

These days, I find myself an aging hunter with some of those same characteristics. In addition, I have more than my share of physical problems. Due to outside forces beyond my control, I must learn to deal with mobility, balance and fatigue issues. Medications help, but my days of following bird dogs for miles have evolved into following them a mile at a time. The determination still exists, but my drivetrain is slipping.

So, I've learned to adapt. A close-working field-bred English cocker spaniel named Buster has helped immensely. I've learned to hunt smarter—hunting the fringes, as I call it. Logging roads have become my best friend. A quarter mile down a logging road, repeat back to the truck. Less-traveled gravel roads, bordering clear-cuts and alder swales, make for firm footing while Buster quarters back and forth within shotgun range. Most hunters drive by miles of prime habitat on their way to access roads leading to deeper cover off the beaten paths.

Out west on the prairies, while chasing pheasants, sharp-tails and Huns, close friends know I make a better poster than driver. I have found hunting two-track prairie roads and ditches with a close-working flushing dog can be very productive. And duck hunting on potholes and beaver ponds from a camo folding chair is a godsend.

Hunting ruffed grouse and woodcock can be a daunting endeavor—for both seasoned and twenty-something hunters alike. But even an old hunter with limitations can enjoy the fruits of the greatest upland hunt around—if he or she recognizes their limitations and learns to hunt the fringes.

Thoughts on Hunting…

Hunters may contemplate why their thoughts on hunting change over the years. If one does not hunt, or perhaps has loved ones who do—do they wonder what makes them tick?

The evolution of a hunter is well documented and, for the most part, follows a predictable trend. The final stages, I suggest—and fear—are deeply influenced more by the physical aging process than the mind. The common thread to all thoughts on this subject gravitate to a diminished urge to kill

The author has learned as he gets older how to reap the rewards of hunting the fringes, walking slowly and enjoying the day.

as we age—and a reflective urge to understand our need to hunt—while stopping to smell the roses from time to time.

Folks much more learned and qualified than I have addressed this very subject, including many a verse in the Bible. Aldo Leopold's classic 1940s "Sky Dance" essay ends, "The woodcock is a living refutation of the theory that the utility of a game bird is to serve as a target, or to pose gracefully on a slice of toast. No one would rather hunt woodcock in October than I, but since learning of the sky dance I find myself calling one or two birds enough. I must be sure that, come April, there be no dearth of dancers in the sunset sky."

And of course, Jose Ortega y Gasset in his "Meditations on Hunting":

> [K]*illing is not the exclusive purpose of hunting.... To the sportsman the death of the game is not what interests him; that is not his purpose. What interests him is everything that he had to do to achieve that death—that is, the hunt. Therefore, what was before only a means to an end is now an end in itself. Death is essential because without it there is no authentic hunting: the killing of the animal is the natural end of the hunt and that goal of hunting itself, not of the hunter. The hunter seeks this death because it is no less than the sign of reality for the whole hunting process. To sum up, one does not hunt in order to kill; on the contrary, one kills in order to have hunted.*

My own personal thoughts—while still a work in progress—lean toward a religious analogy. An individual's philosophy on hunting is not unlike their convictions on religion. When it comes to religious beliefs, the importance does not lie in the denomination of your faith—but simply that you believe. Like religion, one's hunting philosophy is a deep personal conviction. The act of pulling the trigger and ending the life of another living creature borders on spiritual. How your conscience deals with your role in this process is yours and yours alone—if one stays within the letter of the law.

So back to the original question. It matters not to me how many birds you kill any given day, season or lifetime. On the other side of the coin, do not judge my evolving state of mind as a hunter, and I will not judge yours.

For this old hunter, the act of stopping and smelling the roses gets better every day.

About the Author

Ken M. Blomberg's popular outdoor column "Up the Creek" has run for nearly three decades in numerous Wisconsin papers and publications. His first book, also titled *Up the Creek*, was published in 2017. Ken's freelance articles have appeared in many state and national magazines, including *Field & Stream, Pointing Dog Journal, Wing & Shot, Ruffed Grouse Society Magazine, Bird Dog News, Wisconsin Sportsman, Badger Sportsman, Woods and Waters* and *Fur, Fish & Game*. Now retired, Ken writes full time and owns a gun-dog kennel with his wife, Lynda, near Junction City, Wisconsin.

Visit us at
www.historypress.com